STRANGERS NO LONGER

STRANGERS
NO LONGER

Derek Palmer

Foreword by
Derek Worlock

Hodder & Stoughton

LONDON SYDNEY AUCKLAND TORONTO

British Library Cataloguing in Publication Data

Palmer, Derek
    Strangers no longer.
    1. Christian church. Ecumenical movement. Organization
    I. Title
    262.0011
    ISBN 0-340-53823-6

Published by Hodder and Stoughton, a division of Hodder and Stoughton Ltd, Mill Road, Dunton Green, Sevenoaks, Kent TN13 2YA. Editorial Office: 47 Bedford Square, London WC1B 3DP.

Typeset by Medcalf Type Ltd, Bicester
Printed in Great Britain by Clays Ltd, St Ives plc

Contents

Foreword

The decade of the '80s were momentous years on the stage of British ecumenism. They include moments of near despair, such as at the time of the failure of the English Covenant for unity scheme; moments of considerable anxiety, such as the time when the visit of Pope John Paul II was in jeopardy; and moments as at the 1987 Swanwick Conference, full of exciting promise for the future.

Behind such peak moments, however, lie more hidden stories of careful, detailed and deeply taxing labours of discussion, negotiation, preparation. The forerunners of every major event are those who generously undertake this work; and they often remain unsung.

The author of this book is one such labourer in the Lord's vineyard. Here, without in any way singing his own praises, he puts before us some of the less well recorded events of this decade of ecumenism, concentrating largely on the Inter-Church Process 'Not Strangers But Pilgrims', which spans the years 1984–1990. Derek Palmer is well placed to do this, for he was closely involved in the early stages of that Process.

His account rings with the same enthusiasm he brought to the task itself. It is an enthusiasm to involve as many people as possible in these aspects of Church life; an enthusiasm to give to lay people the attention they deserve but do not always receive; an enthusiasm to keep initiatives rooted in the life of the local Church and local community.

This personal view of the journey that has brought the Churches in Britain to the start of a new phase in their history is to be warmly welcomed. I hope it will do more than inform. I, like my Christian-namesake, hope it will enthuse its readers to join together in this pilgrimage so that our joint witness and service in society may be more visibly to the greater glory of God.

DEREK WORLOCK
Archbishop of Liverpool

INTRODUCTION

The Views of Birds and Worms

This book has been written for One Million Readers – but neither the publishers nor I will mind if a few others buy and read it! The Million Readers are those who took part in Lent '86, when together we tried to answer the question, 'What on earth is the Church for?'

The response to that question in 1986 was almost entirely a lay response and gave the unity movement in Britain just what was needed. The good ship 'Ecumenia' had been afloat for over seventy years, but it was a bit stuck in the mud, and needed a fresh tidal wave to get it floating again and give it new direction.

But what has happened since 1986, and what is this new direction? In this book I have tried to write for those tens of thousands of small groups that met throughout England, Scotland and Wales (and in a few more distant places as well), and to tell them the story of 'Not Strangers But Pilgrims' down to its re-launch on September 1st, 1990 under the new banner of 'Churches Together'.

This book is in no sense a 'history' of ecumenism in the 1980s – I am not competent to write such a history, and all of us are too close to these events to be objective about them. This is a personal book by one person who had the great good fortune to be involved at many different levels. In fact for the past forty years I have experienced almost all the joys and the heartbreaks of ecumenism, even though most of my own experience has been only in England.

For part of that time I had a bird's-eye view as from 1985 to 1988 I was one of the Associate Secretaries of 'Not

Strangers But Pilgrims', and also for those four years I
served as the Local Ecumenical Officer of the Church of
England. For seven years before that (1977–84) I had a fairly
wide-ranging view as the founding Secretary of the Kent
Ecumenical Council. So parts of this book come from a
bird's-eye view ranging over a good variety of town and
country scape, and I also had the joy of visiting and taking
part in many ecumenical gatherings and local projects.

But however exciting it is to soar over a wide area and
have a superficial knowledge, one can miss a great deal of
important detail and it may well be that the most helpful
part of this book is the worm's-eye view of one who has
spent most of his ministry at the real grass-roots – down
where it all happens, or should happen.

From my schoolboy days in east Bristol, through to
helping create one of the first Local Ecumenical Projects in
Swindon, I have lived and worked in places where 'Unity
in Christ' was the air we breathed. Most of my early years
in ministry were spent on new housing estates in Bristol
where practising Christians were in a small minority, and
denominations a luxury we could not afford. We were
surrounded by 'post-Christian secular society' but were also
deeply aware of people's need for a living and loving
experience of Jesus Christ and his renewing Church. Our
Gospel was fettered and hindered by controversies of the
past which meant little or nothing to almost everyone we
tried to contact.

I had been born and bred in broad stream Church of
England, and to this day rejoice in my Church which
continues to astonish and ashame me in varying degrees.
But my love and loyalty for my own Church could never
blind me to so much that is good and helpful in other
traditions and other Christian lives I have come to know
and respect. Perhaps if one spent all one's life in a large
'successful' Church one does not need any other Christian
experience, but our young housing-estate Church was not
'successful' and while we struggled to create a new and
simple Christian lifestyle, we were prepared to take
encouragement and advice from any quarter we could get

it. Unity was both desirable and essential if we were to make any impact at all on our raw new community.

I then found that these early lessons were also true in very different circumstances when we moved to Swindon Old Town. Here we had well-attended Churches in a settled though growing town, but we found how much more was possible when Churches pooled Christian resources. Gradually we were learning one of the main lessons that emerged from the thousands of Lent '86 groups: namely that 'to be different is not to be wrong'. Ecumenism now rejoices in the fact that we can worship the One God and Father of our Lord Jesus Christ, in different ways, and we can affirm and hold to our way, without denying the validity of the way of others.

These convictions and experiences launched me into my next phase of ministry in Kent, and at national level, with the 'Not Strangers But Pilgrims' process. During this time I constantly found that my value and help to people was to share with them in very different places the local experiences I had received. G. K. Chesterton rightly said, 'If it isn't local, it isn't real,' and I can only say I agree with him.

So it is that this book has been written with experience as both 'worm' and 'bird'. I am now back again where I belong as a 'worm in the grass-roots'! I have moved to new soil a bit further north and to a slightly cooler climate, but now rejoice in being a Derbyshire man. I have felt compelled to write this book because the story needs telling, and telling with enthusiasm and insight into its relevance 'at all levels and in all places' (the Swanwick Declaration of 1987).

It is good that in September 1990 'Churches Together' will start a new pattern of practical Christian unity, but this will mean little unless it also starts life in every part of our country. That can only be done by local Christians Together.

I hope that the opening chapters will give something of the great joys, sorrows and frustrations that led up to the historic Swanwick Declaration of 1987, and that something of the new hope, ideas and structures described briefly in chapter five will be of interest to most readers. But the heart of the book lies in the final two chapters where 'the worm has turned' and tried to see just what all this Inter-Church Process can really mean at the grass-roots level. If the million of us who played such a big part in Lent '86 and got this mighty enterprise under way, can now take on board the opportunities open to us, the events of the eighties will have a profound effect on the nineties – especially if this new co-operation coincides with an effective 'Decade for Evangelism'.

This then is my view of what has happened, and I must be personally answerable for mistakes, omissions and any offence it may cause. It has been written fairly quickly alongside many joyful and important parochial and family events which have in fact included a re-launch of 'Churches Together in Dronfield' where I now have the joy to serve as rector. Because of this I have not had access to all the files and minutes of the past ten years, but what I have had, and has made this book possible, has been the generous and candid comments of most of my former colleagues – both fellow 'birds' and 'worms'! Each of them has seen an early draft, and as a result hardly a single paragraph has emerged unscathed from their comments – though I hope this does not show too much!

My two fellow Secretaries of 'Not Strangers But Pilgrims' have been of special help to me as they have remained at their posts. Colin Davey is still very much involved in the British Council of Churches (BCC) and now 'Churches Together', and has helped greatly with many factual corrections in the early chapters. Vincent Nichols has throughout been able to combine great Roman Catholic understanding and sensitivity, with an ability to interpret that Church to those of us who are still trying to come to terms with its richness and variety.

Throughout England, and indeed Britain, the name of Hugh Cross is almost synonymous with local ecumenism, and as he comes to the end of his time as Ecumenical Officer for England, and returns to the Baptist ministry, I want to pay a special tribute to his help throughout these years. He is one of the greatest 'birds' but has also always remained a 'worm'! In the book I have acknowledged the help that all of us had from Alastair Haggart (the retired Primus of the Episcopal Church in Scotland), and his comments from both his Scottish and International background have been most canny. I am also indebted to Noel Davies who after many years in ecumenical work in Wales is now the Secretary of CYTUN (Churches Together in Wales). He has kindly corrected some of my worst ignorance of the Welsh scene, and added some helpful insights from that part of our Islands.

My own colleagues in the Church of England Board for Mission and Unity have given me great encouragement and much practical help. Martin Reardon, author of *What on Earth is the Church For?* and in fact my 'boss', at the Board for Mission and Unity (and now Secretary of Churches Together in England) has been a true inspiration to me, and a good deal of his wisdom is here throughout this book. Geoffrey Pearson was another real friend during most of the central events of this book, and now has also returned to the grass-roots in a parish in Liverpool. Much of the early part of chapter seven has come from his wide knowledge of ecumenical mission activity. My successor as Home Secretary (Christopher Drummond) has also read through the script and brought me up to date on much that has happened since I moved away from London.

But all these are 'clergy persons' of one sort or another, and I have tried to write this for lay people, so my final thanks must be to three local lay people who have helped me to simplify ideas and hopefully find a language of the people. Jenny Carpenter (now a near neighbour in Sheffield) is no ordinary lay person having been a Vice President of the Methodist Conference and a fellow worker right through the Inter-Church Process, but she has always been essentially a 'lay voice' and a mighty one at that! Eileen Brady has been the Secretary of the Dronfield Council of Churches for many years and as a member of the United Reformed Church has in her time played almost every part that can be played on the local ecumenical scene.

My third 'lay view' is a very special and important one;

Cecilie, my wife, has not only read and re-read every word, and tried to teach me grammar, but much more importantly has shared almost all the experiences of this book and given me the love and encouragement to make much of it possible.

My final word of thanks goes to the Rt Rev Derek Worlock, Archbishop of Liverpool, who has generously written the Foreword. I never had any doubt that he was the person I hoped would agree to write it. Throughout his time in Liverpool and in 'Not Strangers But Pilgrims' he has played a bridging role that has won great love and admiration. I personally owe him a great deal and am glad to be able to say so now.

But may I end this Introduction on a slightly facetious note? It is often the custom of authors to dedicate a book to someone 'without whom this book could not have been written'. If this is so then I dedicate it to my Amstrad PCW 9512 without whom this book couldn't have been written and re-written and re-written . . .

1

Walking hand in hand – but where to?

Most years are fixed in our minds by an important personal event such as the birth of a child, a new job or a marriage. But for Britain, 1982 is remembered as the year we went and fought over a small island at the bottom of most of our atlases. It was the year of the Falklands conflict.

For the Christian Church, too, it was a memorable year and seems the right place to start from when we consider where the Churches of Britain stand at the start of the nineties.

The Churches' quest for unity is linked with the Falklands conflict because one of the main religious events of that year nearly did not take place as a direct result of it. The planned visit of the Pope to Britain hung in the balance until just a few days before he arrived, because the minds of so many were preoccupied with Goose Green and the *Belgrano*, and because the Pope himself had to decide whether it was right for him as a 'messenger of peace' to visit a country in a virtual state of declared war. Eventually the Pope gave an understanding that he would later visit Argentina, and invited British and Argentinian Catholics to celebrate a Mass of Reconciliation with him in Rome on the eve of his visit to Britain.

Papal Visit

Great courage was needed on the part of both the Roman

Catholic Church here, and the Papacy in Rome to agree that the visit should go ahead, and none could doubt that the decision was truly 'a historic one'. The first visit of a Pope to these shores, and that at a time of considerable distress and perplexity. The world was getting used to a peripatetic Pope who seemed to enjoy nothing more than kissing foreign tarmac, but so far most of his visits were to Catholic lands. Britain had a growing Catholic population but in many of its beliefs and prejudices it was still largely Protestant – even if now more by tradition than conviction.

The visit was designed to be a pastoral one to the Catholic Church in the mainland of Britain, but some Roman Catholics, including many leaders, were hoping also to see some realisation of the ecumenical dreams they had after the National Pastoral Congress at Liverpool in May 1980. The visit certainly fulfilled its pastoral role and his visits to Roman Catholics in England, Scotland and Wales brought great crowds to meet him.

But looking back on the visit of Pope John Paul II, there can be little doubt that the most memorable part of his programme was the visit to Canterbury Cathedral. This was not just any Cathedral but the heart of the world-wide Anglican Communion.

As one who was in the Cathedral on that day it seemed almost unbelievable that it was actually happening and we were taking part in such a deeply symbolic event which must herald great changes. Adrian Hastings in his book (*A History of English Christianity*, page 646) makes special mention of the reading of the Gospel by the Pope, and the Primate reading the Epistle; but for me it was the Pope, the Archbishop and the Moderator of the Free Church Federal Council (Rev Kenneth Greet) kneeling together to reaffirm their common baptismal vows which filled me with joy and hope. Pope John Paul II made its meaning quite clear in his address:

In a few moments we will renew our baptismal vows together. We intend to perform this ritual, which we share in common as Anglicans and Catholics and other

Christians, as a clear testimony to the One Sacrament of Baptism by which we have been joined to Christ. Christ's promise gives us confidence in the power of the Holy Spirit to heal divisions introduced into the Church in the course of centuries. In this way the renewal of our baptismal vows will become a pledge to do all in our power to co-operate with the grace of the Holy Spirit, who alone can lead us to the day when we will profess the fullness of our faith together.

In these words, and in the symbolic actions, there was a basis on which we could build. In our baptism in Christ, we had something that was shared not only by the leaders of the denominations, but by the millions of ordinary Church members who were 'one in Christ' and who were the Body of Christ.

If Canterbury was the greatest experience of that visit, the greatest quote came from Pope John Paul II in Glasgow when he addressed a question to a vast crowd of Catholics and other Christians as well, 'For the future can we not make our pilgrimage together, hand in hand?' These two images of pilgrimage and walking hand in hand – the first implying movement and the second true love and courtship were powerful ones to project in our land, especially saying it in Scotland.

Theological Progress

The year 1982 was also an important one for the Anglican and Roman Catholic theologians who, after the final Windsor statement of 1981 on authority within the Church, were able to publish the full report of ARCIC I (Anglican Roman Catholic International Commission). It tackled many of the thorniest questions on the Eucharist, Ministry, and Authority. Eleven years of patient meetings (mostly residential) by this small group found that much that divided them lay in their different histories and languages. While the road ahead would be arduous and contain many pitfalls and blind alleys, the theological barriers were crumbling, and the misunderstandings and ignorances were being shown up for what they were – controversies of the past which could be creatively unpacked and then used by Christians today facing this increasingly secular age.

But if ARCIC I had taken eleven years of hard work, what of that other document that also first saw the light of day in 1982? In an age which loves initials (sometimes to show familiarity rather than knowledge!) ARCIC I had its companion in BEM. 'Baptism, Eucharist and Ministry' had its roots in the Faith and Order Movement, itself part of the gestation period of the World Council of Churches. For over fifty years it had brought together the theologians of the world, including the Orthodox, and later the Roman Catholic. It was in this setting that they met with Baptists, Reformed, Anglicans, Lutherans and Methodists and with their brothers and sisters from the burgeoning Churches of Africa, Asia and more lately South America. They found a considerable ignorance of each other's theological positions, but as they met over the years they were able to arrive at a remarkable convergence of understanding on many issues.

Northern traditionalism came face to face with the often livelier and more charismatic Churches of the South. While many had thought of these lands only as 'missionary lands', the theologians of the North were finding much to learn from the newer Christians of the rapidly developing Churches of the South. The European and American Church was giving way to the world-wide Church, and for some this was a painful process. As they met many found their basic assumptions challenged on a variety of religious, social and political issues. It is no accident that the final BEM report was issued from a conference at the city of Lima in South America. Such is the ignorance of this part of the world that some were known to ask 'What do the initials LIMA stand for?'

The year 1982 was a bumper one for the theologians, and eight years later we are still trying to come to terms with what they are saying to us. When they are together the theologians of the world are able to walk hand in hand and find much common ground, but sometimes they forget this experience when they return to their own denominational or national groups. But this is a common experience which can affect any one of us at every level of Church life and it can be our experience, too, when we come back from our Council of Churches to the 'really important' matters of the church roof, the new hymn book, or whose turn it is to sweep up after the playgroup have used the church hall!

Failure of Thirty Years of Unity Talks

So the year 1982 began well for those concerned for the unity of the Church, but that is not the whole story, for it also brought failure after thirty years of unity talks in England.

The origins of these talks can be traced to November 23rd, 1946 and the immediate post-war years when the Archbishop of Canterbury (the Rt Rev Geoffrey Fisher) made his main contribution to ecumenism. In a notable sermon delivered from the pulpit of Great St Mary's, Cambridge, he invited the English Free Churches (the negative word Nonconformist was beginning to give way to this more positive title by then) to 'take episcopacy into their own system'. It was hardly a scheme for reunion and though it seemed to be a possible way forward towards mutual recognition of ministries, what emerged from it was eventually rejected by Dr Fisher himself.

As in the First World War, the experiences of the troops in the front line convinced many that the divisions of Church life mattered less than they had thought, so in the Second World War the civilian population in the Anderson shelters or sleeping in the tube stations, found the same. What mattered was a faith in God, and others matters seemed secondary.

So the war had brought more relaxed relationships between Churches and by 1946 the Free Churches were associated with Anglicans and the Church of Scotland through the newly formed British Council of Churches, which began life in 1942. This coming together of the

Churches in Britain was only part of the long history which had led up to the forming of the British Council of Churches. From its inception the Council had not only sought to hold together the denominations but the Churches of the four nations that it contained as well.

After 1946 there was a feeling that the time was right for some advance in Christian unity, away from the often arid squabbles over Religious Education and Establishment – hence the Archbishop's Cambridge sermon. The Free Churches in England, quite understandably, took their time in answering the Archbishop, and in the end the only one to set up formal conversations was the Methodist Church. It was by far the biggest of the English Free Churches and was itself the result of internal reunion in 1932, and had always tried to keep a close relationship with the Church of England. So began the long and tortuous story of the Anglican–Methodist Conversations. In the end all that was produced was much talk, many meetings, long reports and growing frustration. Sufficient to say that the Church which made the suggestion was not itself prepared to accept the final proposals that emerged, and twice rejected the proposed scheme largely because of the acceptance of the ordination of those not episcopally ordained. Finally in 1972, despite the passionate pleading of Archbishop Michael Ramsay, the General Synod of the Church of England closed the door on the scheme and left Methodists bewildered and hurt, and many Anglicans bitter and angry. The effect on the Methodist Church of this double rejection was profound and I was part of the Commission which had the sad task of burying the body, and trying to save a few mementoes for the future. It was not a happy task for any of us.

But all was not gloom, and in the same year (1972), two Churches which had not accepted the Archbishop's ill-fated invitation achieved organic unity. Out of the Congregational Church and the Presbyterian Church of England came the new United Reformed Church. It was a Church which saw itself as provisional in the hope that it could be a vehicle for further reunion, and in 1981 it merged with the Churches of Christ. This second union was important for two reasons. First, the latter was a Church which only practised 'Believers Baptism', whereas the URC was one where infants were baptised, and secondly, it meant that the URC now had a small but significant membership in Scotland. In Scotland the unity talks between the Anglicans and Presbyterians fared, if anything, worse than similar talks in England.

The final move in this story of the failure of unity talks began in the mid-seventies when, on the initiative of the URC, ten propositions were put to all the Churches in England asking if these could be the basis for further unity talks. This time the Roman Catholic Church, in its post Vatican II mood, was included in the invitation. This could not have happened before, because till then reunion was thought of mainly in terms of Anglican and Free Church unity. This, in fact, was what had split the Church of England throughout this period. Some wanted and worked for such unity with the Free Churches, but others seemed to be pulling in a totally different direction and (despite very little encouragement from Rome or even from Westminster) saw reunion with Rome as the only worthwhile goal. Even to begin considering some form of unity between all the major Christian groupings in this land was an audacious thought.

The Church of England rather reluctantly girded its loins to try again, as did the rejected Methodist Church. But this time they were joined by the United Reformed Church, the Moravian Church and indeed some Baptists. The Roman Catholic response was a qualified 'no', as was the main line Baptist Union response, but they offered goodwill and prayerful support to those who felt they could go ahead and appointed 'observers' to the Council for Covenanting. The presence of such observers and their 'observations' were in fact most helpful and encouraging.

The Churches' Council for Covenanting quickly got down to the task of seeing if a national covenant between the various Churches was possible, and in two years a report was ready which outlined a way in which the various Churches could recognise each other and share ministry.

Some of the lessons of the previous rounds of talks had been learnt, and I was one of the Church of England members of the Covenanting Council. We seemed to make progress face to face, but as with the world's theologians we regressed when we got back to our own constituencies and 'parties'.

But now the question of women's ordination came into the debate, and may have been one reason why, in July 1982, the General Synod of the Church of England put the final nail in the coffin of English unity talks. Despite the leadership of most of the bishops and the acceptance of many laity, the House of Clergy was found to include a sufficient number opposed to the Covenant for it to be rejected. And this despite the fact that the other Churches had accepted it with the required majority and were prepared to make much greater changes than the Church of England would be called upon to make.

So the year 1982, which had started so well for ecumenical enthusiasts, faltered badly in the middle, and over a quarter of a century of hard slog, much prayer and millions of words, written and spoken, came to a shuddering halt. For many there was a special sadness and sorrow caused by the sudden death of the Bishop of Guildford (the Rt Rev David Brown) who had led the Church of England members of the Covenanting Council.

There were no unity talks anywhere in England. In Wales however the implications of the 1975 Covenant were being further developed and in Scotland the Multilateral Conversations continued; but in the main the high hopes of the 1964 Nottingham Faith and Order Conference had not been realised.

So for some the summer of 1982 brought great sorrow and bitterness; there were still deep divisions on important matters, but need these have stopped the undoubted progress that had been made? To quote the veteran Methodist ecumenist Rupert Davies, 'Some have argued that the rejections were the will of God, eccentrically disclosed to a minority of Anglican clergy, a few bishops, and less than a quarter of the Methodist Conference. This view is unsustainable in the light of the dire consequences for all the Churches involved' (*Church Times*, October 6th, 1989).

Was it high principle, or fear, that brought twenty-five years work to a halt? It is hard to escape the conviction that it was fear of change, and a lack of faith in a 'pilgrimage God'. Bishop Kenneth Woollcombe's review of the Covenant published later called it 'a lack of will'.

The failure of Covenant in 1982 can hardly be called a blessing in disguise, as some have claimed, because a breakthrough then would have brought much ecumenical progress and encouragement and transformed the situation. However, clearly God is now seeking to show us another way forward as this book will try to show. But it would take a brave person to say that this was God's will for his divided Church all along. Rather it reveals the timidity of God's people and our love of the status quo despite which he continues to love and lead us.

Grass-Roots Growth

But is that the whole story of the year 1982; a papal visit, a theological report, and a vote in General Synod? For those who see history as the big events, it may have been, but for most Christians in Britain they were just items in the serious or Church newspapers, and were simply 'them up there, going on'.

Throughout the period of the unity talks, I had the good fortune to be working first in Swindon and later in Kent, where unity did not rely on Church decisions at the top but on the willingness of local Christians to get on with each other, and doing together some of the things which others seemed to find hard even to contemplate as possible.

If the grass-roots movement must have an official birthday it would be 1964 at the British Council of Churches Faith and Order Conference at Nottingham University, which has already been referred to above. But there were signs of it much earlier than that. In 1944 I worshipped in a Local Ecumenical Project twenty years before the term was ever thought of. It was in war-blitzed east Bristol where the local vicar, the Rev Mervyn Stockwood, and his curate, the Rev John Robinson, united with the local Methodist Minister, the Rev Donald Rose, in the Redfield United Front. It was here that, as a 'low Anglican', I first smelt incense, but more importantly learnt that the Church of England was not the only Church in this land. To this day I rejoice in my schoolboy membership of the United Front and its combined Youth Club.

Bristol can rightly claim its place in the ecumenical story, but it was not alone. It was the Nottingham Conference of 1964, though, which first brought together the striving experiments of local ecumenism, and the structures of the Churches themselves. Nottingham '64 is now usually identified with a failure since, in a rush of blood to the head, delegates dared to hope that reunion in Britain would come by Easter Day 1980. They were wrong in that hope, but right on other things. Three of their decisions have gone some way to compensate for the Easter Day failure. One was to seek for united Theological Colleges so that the clergy and ministers who seemed so ignorant of each other, could train together. The Anglican–Methodist Theological College, 'The Queen's College, Birmingham' was the most direct fruit of this, as was the ecumenical broadening of the non-residential training such as the Southwark, and North West Ordination Courses. The second was the setting up of the discussions in Wales that led to the 1975 Covenant. The final resolution was even more far-reaching; this was to allow the setting up of Areas of Ecumenical Experiment, later to be called Local Ecumenical Projects (LEPs for the lovers of initials).

Local Ecumenical Projects

The original title, Areas of Ecumenical Experiment, described the early ones well. 'At Nottingham many people argued that changing patterns in society would demand new patterns from the Churches, not least in response to the increasing secularism in British society. It was this missionary purpose that lay behind the resolution about areas of ecumenical experiment. What few people realised was that the resolution would lead rapidly to a changed atmosphere in the sharing of ministry and mission and that this would require church rules and customs to be adapted to meet the new situation' (John Matthews, *The Unity Scene*, BCC, 1985, page 85).

In 1964 there was a confident mood that soon the Anglican and Methodist Churches at least would be one, and so some places should be encouraged to operate ahead of the main body, and find out what the possibilities were and where the problems lay.

After Nottingham 1964, each denomination had to consider how far it could really let areas experiment; how far could it allow them to bend rules, or break them in private, while the Churches themselves were still divided? It is important to remember, for instance, that at this time (the late sixties and early seventies), the Church of England did not allow non-Anglicans to receive Communion at their altars. Canon B15a, which allowed this, was agreed to by the General Synod in the very year in which the Anglican Methodist scheme was finally rejected by it. Some Free Church Christians are still unaware of this change, even now!

But in some dioceses of the Church of England (and again honour must go to Bristol where the ecumenical experience and leadership of Bishop Oliver Tomkins was so important) it was agreed that rules could be broken or bent because soon the rules would be changed. To oversee these new experiments a Regional Sponsoring Body was set up, comprising only the 'uniting Anglican and Methodist Churches'. In time Baptist and URC and then Roman Catholics have been added. The theory was that in new areas and especially on the new housing estates which were ringing our large cities, a single building be erected for several denominations to share. The first breakthrough in the law came when the Sharing of Church Buildings Act was passed in 1969 and gave some legality to the 'Ecumenical Church'. But a single shared building did not always mean much, and to this day there are congregations sharing a building, but little else.

Such bodies as the New Town Ministers' Association encouraged clergy and ministers to take every opportunity to push the Sponsoring Bodies to their limits, and to start experimenting in any way possible. In a small book I wrote in 1963 (while working on a Bristol housing estate), I stated, 'Reunion is coming to this country, and if we are not to wait till whole denominations are reunited, the new communities represent the best possible field for bold and prayerful experiment by the denominations' (*All Things New*, Mowbrays, 1963). That was the confidence of the sixties and though the first part of my statement has not yet been fulfilled, it expresses the conviction that experiments must take place if there was to be any more general advance.

Each LEP had either its own or a corporate Sponsoring Body, but the LEPs frightened the Church leaders by continually asking questions that they could not answer. Joint communion services where all communicated of right were accepted in most places; confirmations where the bishop and appropriate ministers of the other Churches jointly laid-on hands and gave the right hand of fellowship in some; and a sharing of ministries so that the full ministry of the participating denominations were recognised and accepted within the Project itself in a few. But there were marked variations from one part of the country to another and some considerable confusion at all levels.

Predominantly Anglican and Methodist at the start, Baptist and United Reformed Churches and others also joined, and soon there were three hundred 'experiments' and they began to have a voice. In most places the voice was saying things that the majority was not ready to accept, and so the frustration grew.

Soon the LEPs in new housing estates and new towns like Hemel Hempstead, Telford, Stevenage and Harlow were joined by another type of Local Ecumenical Project. Harking back to the war-time east Bristol experiment, these came in the form we now call a 'Local Covenant', which brought together, by voluntary local agreement, existing congregations but usually still maintaining their separate buildings. Some groups came together because of their smallness and found strength in joining in one or more buildings. Others, however, came to local unity because of a conviction that the disunity of the Church was hindering the proclamation of the Good News of Jesus Christ. They were concerned that Churches spoke of peace, harmony and love, but showed a different face in practice.

The expanding Wiltshire town of Swindon was one place where this was considered very carefully, and under the leadership of the Rt Rev Freddie Temple (then Archdeacon of Swindon) a town plan was accepted which grouped existing, and proposed Churches, into seven geographical areas. Not all took root, but most did and still continue to grow. These larger and perhaps more powerful LEPs, continued to ask awkward questions of Church leaders. Sometimes the leaders showed some sympathy but not much understanding of the frustrations of places where the growing local unity was becoming more important than denominational loyalties. These feelings could be contained, as long as a hope could be held out that these problems would be resolved when the Anglican–Methodist scheme came about.

But when the scheme was finally rejected there was a sense of betrayal. The LEPs had been asked to experiment and now felt disowned. I remember asking in the General Synod, 'Seeing our parents have failed to get married, what does that make us who live in the LEPs?'

However, we were assured of our 'legitimacy', and a body with even more strange initials, CCLEPE (Consultative Committee for Local Ecumenical Projects in England) was set up. In view of the growing number of Roman Catholic Churches now becoming part of Local Covenants (such as the one at Edenbridge in Kent), the Roman Catholic Church became a full and active member of it from its inception. So the LEPs began asking CCLEPE the impossible questions that had previously gone to the local Sponsoring Bodies! The annual Swanwick conferences of the growing number of LEPs (four hundred by the end of the seventies) became angry places, and bishops felt it safer to visit in pairs, and even archbishops had rough handling.

The existence of so much positive, but frustrated local ecumenism, encouraged, and perhaps forced, the setting up of the Churches' Council for Covenanting, and also brought urgency to its workings. In the early days of local ecumenism (in which local Councils of Churches also played an important role), the clergy and ministers took a leading part, but as the number of projects grew and became established, so the lay voice became stronger. Lay people in LEPs could not understand how the local experience of fruitful unity was not being accepted everywhere with joy, rather than with restrictions.

Wise heads were needed to keep some LEPs in fellowship with their own parent bodies, and in some cases this tragically failed. But in the main, lay and ordained men and women stayed and fought hard for the wider vision that the Covenant stood for. At the same time they recognised that, though the Roman Catholic Church was only an observer on the Covenanting Council, it was now taking part in a growing number of LEPs, even if on a more sharply defined and restricted basis. The name of Thamesmead was being mentioned as a place where exciting things were happening. Anglicans, Roman Catholics, Methodists and United Reformed Churches were sharing in one new building, and much else as well, in this expanding south-east London township.

In the end the rejection of the Covenant in 1982 was bitterly resented by many as a second betrayal of the living experience of tens of thousands of local Christians. Once again, members of the Church of England in LEPs tried to explain to their fellow members of other traditions how this had happened and their deep sense of shame; apologies were made, tears were shed, angry letters were written but now there seemed nowhere else to go.

Once again the LEPs were 'living in sin', in the eyes of their denominations, but in love and joy in their own eyes, and in the eyes of those outside the Church, who had begun to see that Christians of different denominations could live together in harmony, and then reach out in common mission.

And so 1982 was a very mixed year for ecumenical hopes. It had begun on a 'high' in Canterbury and fell to a 'low' in over five hundred official LEPs, and many more unofficial ones as well. The cry was 'What else can we do? Where do we go from here? We wish to walk hand in hand, but where to?'

2

Birth of a Process

Following the traumatic events of 1982 it was clear that if there was to be any advance in Christian unity in Britain, it had to come from a new and different source. The ecumenical leaders were, in the main, dispirited after what seemed like twenty-five wasted years, and the LEPs, though continuing to grow in numbers, felt lost and disowned.

As after the failure of the Anglican-Methodist talks, the General Synod of the Church of England tried to soften the blow of its rejection of the Covenant, and this time set up a working party under the Bishop of Derby (the Rt Rev Cyril Bowles) to explore new ways by which the Church of England could further local ecumenism. This working party report finally produced the 1988 Ecumenical Canons which have gone some way to helping the local situation, as we shall see in chapter six. But this was little more than the Church of England trying to bolt the stable door after a large number of horses had learnt to roam far and wide!

At the beginning of 1983 the only course open to the Churches was to start with the positive successes of 1982, and build up a new and different initiative based partly on the visit of the Pope to Britain, partly on the encouraging theological advances, and partly on the growing number of LEPs. The Roman Catholic Church, though a member of many local Councils of Churches and a growing number of Local Covenants (following the Catholic publication in 1978 of the Ecumenical Commission of England and Wales report *Local Covenants*), was not a member of the British Council of Churches itself. While they had often been invited, the Catholic bishops felt unable to join the present structure, and there was a growing feeling amongst some other Church leaders as well, that the BCC was becoming tired and needed a new approach for a new era, with or without the Roman Catholics.

So in May 1983 there was a return visit to Rome led by the Primus of the Scottish Episcopal Church (the Rt Rev Alastair Haggart) and made up of BCC and Roman Catholic leaders. They explored what steps could be taken to give expression to these feelings, and at the same time find out what could be done to bring about closer working together, even if full unity itself was not yet possible. From these tentative steps came the Inter-Church Process 'Not Strangers But Pilgrims', a somewhat strange but none-the-less expressive title of the truth about ecumenical relations in Britain and Ireland, and the stage they had reached.

David Winter writes in his book *Battered Bride* (Monarch, 1988):

> In the United Kingdom and especially in England, there is a generally friendly atmosphere between the Churches, reflected at every level. Bishops and Area Superintendents and Moderators meet regularly in most places, but so do the clergy and lay people. The difference from thirty years ago, for those of us who can remember, is striking. I like to feel that religious broadcasting, which introduces people to worship and beliefs of other Christians in a completely non-threatening context has contributed to this. One feels that in the end this new atmosphere must produce visible results, though organisational unity, certainly between those Churches with 'catholic' order and priesthood and the others may be a long way off. (page 61)

The Churches were 'not strangers' but they still had a long way to go, and the image of 'pilgrims' walking 'hand in hand together' best expressed the sometime seemingly contradictory relationships which had emerged over the past twenty years, and also picked up Pope John Paul's challenge at Glasgow.

Before we trace the story of the Inter-Church Process itself it would be wise to put this fairly narrow ecclesiastical process into the wider setting of British Church life as a whole as it was in 1983. The leaders of the Churches and indeed their members, were faced by a variety of problems and opportunities, some of which were old but others were very new. In the main they can be classified under five headings:

1. The failure of the unity talks
2. The realisation that Britain was now a mission field
3. The failure to integrate the new 'black-led' Churches in England
4. The growing number of people of other faiths in our cities
5. The considerable loss of people from the traditional Churches to 'House Churches'

These issues were not all of equal importance to every Church, but in the main they were shared by all Churches in England, and some of them in Wales and Scotland as well. From the start it was recognised that the situation in Ireland was so different that a full participation by all the Churches was very unlikely, and this proved to be the case.

The Failure of Unity Talks

As we have seen in chapter one, the unity movement had so far not delivered the goods: the front line troops were tired, the generals and staff officers were bewildered, and some at all levels had lost heart. It was true that ARCIC and similar international talks were producing some remarkable reports, but these cut little ice at local level where there was a growing feeling that the Churches were big on talk, but small on results.

Something had to be done to recruit new enthusiasts who

would lift spirits and provide a new impetus, if the unity movement was to be got going again after the failures in 1982. At this stage no one guessed what a powerful new force would be unleashed by lay people through Lent '86, but something was certainly going to be needed to put new heart into local Churches and through them, the Church leaders. Even 'Ecumaniacs' get disheartened and need vision and encouragement!

We are a Mission Field

The other main driving force in getting the Inter-Church Process launched was the recognition that Britain itself was now a mission field. Complacency could not stand up to the statistical decline in almost every one of the main denominations. It was not just in Church attendance that the problem lay; whole areas of national life such as education, youth work and the caring agencies were losing their Christian content and influence. Some still called Britain a Christian country, but others talked of living in a 'post-Christian culture'. While Scotland could point to higher average Church attendance than England or Wales, no Church could view the situation with equanimity. There was a sharp decline in Welsh Free Churches, and most of the English Churches found little comfort in their annual statistics.

In England all the historic Free Churches, except for the Baptists, had lost ground and though the Roman Catholics still seemed to have full congregations, their statistics spoke of many lapsed members, and a shortage of vocations made worse by an ageing clergy in need of fresh blood. Exact figures are hard to come by, but in England about twelve per cent of the population were active in Church membership at the start of the eighties. This meant just under six million active Christians, made up of about two million communicant members of the Church of England, two million practising Roman Catholics, and under two million in the other Churches. Scotland was able to achieve figures nearer to twenty per cent, but Wales overall was a little behind England. It will be interesting to see if the 1989 English Church Census produces very different figures from the ones above.

These are still large numbers of people, and should not, of themselves, cause depression. Any political party, sporting group or trade union which could week by week assemble six million people, would be overjoyed. But the reality is that six million is a much smaller figure than ever before, and even more disturbing is their uneven spread in terms of age and geography. Despite excellent youth organisations such as the Methodist Association of Youth Clubs, the average age of some congregations is elderly, and some are mainly female. Both the elderly and women play a vital part in the life of the Church, but men and young people are also essential to the continuity of it.

Equally worrying is the uneven geographical and social spread of the Churches. While it may be true of the Church of England, as Bishop Ted Wickham wrote some years ago from his experience in the field of industrial mission, 'It is not so much that we have lost the working class, but that we have never had them', the fact remains that in large tracts of our towns and cities and their surrounding estates, it would be difficult to find even one per cent of Church attenders, let alone twelve per cent.

Partly caused by traditional hostility to established Church privilege and wealth, but accelerated by the break up of traditional communities through the building of new estates and towns, the Church of England and the Free Churches now have little presence in many inner cities and 'EastEnds'. And this despite often heroic work by some priests and ministers, and faithful laity who have preserved something of the true Christian working class culture. It is surely no accident, that alongside 'Not Strangers But Pilgrims' there has been the launch of such initiatives as the Methodist Mission Alongside the Poor, and more recently the Church of England's Church Urban Fund.

This is an uncomfortable picture, and some Churches, in reasonably prosperous towns and suburbs, wish that all this talk would go away, and they could be left to get on with their own seemingly 'successful Church life'. It is still easier to raise funds for missions in Asia or Africa, than for the centre of the nearest city, even though many of its members work in the city where they encounter the problems every day. This therefore meant that any new ecumenical impetus would need to be as much about evangelism, as ecumenism. The luxury of having two separate structures, attitudes and enthusiasms − one for ecumenism and the other for evangelism, must go and go quickly. While the Churches of the northern hemisphere seem to be in decline, in the South it is a different story. It is clear that the Roman Catholic worldwide initiative in making the 1990s a Decade of Evangelisation, and the 1988 Lambeth Conference call for a Decade of Evangelism, were similar approaches which must be urgently shared by all Churches together. Nothing less than the total resources of all the Churches was needed if any real impression was to be made on a country which was drifting further and further away from its Christian traditions and the living Gospel of Jesus Christ.

The Integration of the 'Black-Led' Churches

We now live in 'one world' and no longer do 'black' Christians just live in Africa, 'white' ones in Europe and so called 'yellow' ones in the Far East. We are all now mixed up in every land and the emergence, growth and vitality of the so-called 'black-led' Churches is a major factor of Church life in England, but less so in Wales and even less in Scotland. The term 'black-led' is an unsatisfactory title for these new Churches, but it has come into use recently because in addition there are also many black people who have remained in the traditional denominations even though these Churches are overwhelmingly 'white-led'.

As with our Urban Priority Areas, many Church-goers in England have little idea of how these new British Churches came to birth, or even more sadly, why they came to birth:

By the end of the sixties there were forty or more different Churches, mostly West Indian, which had sprung up in England in the wake of the immigration. Some were very small but a few had many thousands of practising members. While all were not Pentecostal the largest were. The New Testament Church of God had twenty-three congregations in Britain in 1964 and sixty-one two years later. Immigrants found the existing Churches mostly staid, elderly and very little interested in them. They had been Anglicans, Baptists and Roman Catholics in Jamaica, but the great majority quickly ceased to be so in Britain (Hastings, *A History of English Christianity, op.cit.*, page 553).

The appalling failure of the Churches to welcome their members from the Caribbean was a sin which caused enormous hurt and damage which is still with us.

The Mother Country was a sad disappointment to many immigrants, especially as some came here seeing our country as the home of the Christian missions that had brought them to faith. But their cold reception soon removed the concept of England as a Christian country:

For the most part congregations felt that they had done their duty if they allowed 'our West Indian friends' to use the Church hall for worship 'in their customary exuberant style'. It is not surprising that in due course these groups moved further and further away from the mainstream Churches, forming distinct congregations and eventually separate denominations. By the late 1970s these new groups were so numerous, influential and self-confident that they could begin to re-establish relationships with the older Churches on terms of parity (David Winter, *Battered Bride, op.cit.*, page 155).

Certainly the growth of these Churches in the past twenty years has become a major factor in English Church life in the main conurbations. Few English cities are without large black Christian congregations, many of them still meeting in hired Church halls, or worshipping in very sub-standard

premises. The coolness and formality that was so off-putting
to the first immigrants in English Churches, has been
replaced in their own fellowships by a warmth and
spontaneity that can be overpowering to those not used to
their freer way of worship. The *Songs of Praise* from
Southwark Cathedral, televised in 1987, contributed entirely
by London Gospel Choirs and black congregations, was an
eye-opener to many, and proved to be one of the most
popular broadcasts. The black-led Churches had come of
age, and were now being taken seriously alongside the other
Churches.

It has not been easy, for the black-led Churches
maintained their own way of life. As I have found on a
number of occasions, white people were made welcome at
their services, but the leadership stayed firmly in black
hands. The Selly Oak colleges in Birmingham set up a black
and white pastors' weekend training course, which helped
those who were able to take part in them, and played an
important role in helping to build bridges of theological and
personal understanding.

Some local Councils of Churches began to make overtures
of friendship but not everyone realised what problems were
created for black Christians by white styles of leadership
and concepts of co-operation. White superiority, which has
sometimes marred the history of our Missionary Societies,
can still be seen and experienced in our own country in all
walks of life, including the Church itself. To this has to be
added the often bitter memories of their first 'Christian'
reception in this country, so it is not surprising that many
black Christians are somewhat wary of these new advances.

Another problem for black pastors' participation in local
ecumenical life was that most of them had to be self-
supporting through secular work, and yet most clergy and
ministers' fraternals took place during the day at times
convenient for full-time clergy. Without adjustments by the
organisers of such gatherings (and this affects all non-
stipendiary clergy as well) there is a lack of opportunity to
build up relationships on which good local co-operation
normally depends.

At the national level a number of African and Afro-Caribbean Churches and their leaders were beginning to work with the British Council of Churches and the Evangelical Alliance, but many others resisted such involvement. But there was also a growing recognition in the white Churches that, although they came from a different culture, this very difference was what many English Churches needed to complement their seeming reserve.

This was certainly an important consideration in the setting up of the Inter-Church Process in 1983, and it is encouraging to note that out of the thirty-six Churches which participated in its launch no less than nine were black-led Churches. Here was a powerful and vocal group of Christians, whose contribution must be valued and included in any coming together to share and further the Gospel of Jesus Christ in Britain.

Growth of Other Faiths

People living in Britain were not only conscious of black Christians, but of the growing number of people of other faiths now living in our cities. There were now tens of thousands of British people who were God fearing, but who were not Christians. How do we come to terms with this multi-faith society? It was known that large parts of Leicester had many of Hindu faith; Southall of Sikhs and Hindus; Oldham, Rochdale and Bradford of Muslims, and Birmingham had growing numbers of most of these religious communities which were new to Britain in any large numbers. But it was only gradually that the Churches in and outside these areas came to terms with the fact that these people held to a religious belief and way of life and practice just as strongly, or even more strongly, than Christians do. It was true that the Jewish community in Leeds and North London and in smaller groups elsewhere, had been here for centuries, but they had become somewhat better assimilated because their background had been mainly European.

When 'other religions' lived in far off lands, they were all too often seen as heathen 'bowing down to wood and stone', and the Churches thought they knew how to handle the situation. But many were slow to realise that these people were now our neighbours living in our towns and cities, and that as fellow citizens we had to live with them and learn to respect their views.

One of the tragedies of the late sixties and seventies is that the Churches were not more alive to what was happening in many of our inner-city schools.

Christians in the teaching profession came face to face with 'other faiths' twenty years before Salman Rushdie forced these issues on everyone else. The problem of integrating children of four or five different religions into one school assembly, and making it both meaningful and constructive, had forced teachers into areas of inter-faith work long before most clergy and theologians were fully aware of the problems.

Had we listened to many of our returned missionaries (such as Archbishop George Appleton) who had lived in this situation in India and other places, we would have known that antagonism and superiority must be replaced by respect and dialogue. Frequently those who are firmest in their belief in the unique revelation of God in Jesus Christ, are also those who love and respect others whose knowledge of God has come to them through other revelations and cultures.

Christians in this country have been perplexed by experiencing this rapid mixing of the world's religions. This is illustrated by one parish in Birmingham where the vicar of a fairly small united Anglican, Methodist and United Reformed Church told me that in his inner-city parish there were thirty-four places of worship, and only three others were Christian!

In Britain, as in many other countries, Christians, Muslims, Hindus and people of other faiths, work together in the same shops, offices and factories, study together in the same schools and colleges, travel on the same buses and trains, work together in the same hospitals, pay the same taxes and are represented by the same Members of Parliament. People find this religious and cultural mixture a novel and bewildering experience. Not only Christians, but people of other faiths as well, find it strange to work as colleagues or be neighbours with people who hold different beliefs, and observe different customs, who keep different religious festivals and holidays, and who profess allegiance to different religious teachers. Sometimes Christians admire the devotion and loyalty to their faith of those of other religions . . . but more often differences and strangeness divide and alienate the different religious communities (*Towards a Theology for Inter-Faith Dialogue*, a report produced by the Inter-Faith Consultative Group of the Church of England Board for Mission and Unity, 1984).

The fact that theologians in the Churches were discussing this showed how great was the concern, and the above report, although largely descriptive of a variety of theological views, itself stirred some considerable controversy. Clearly the religions of the world can no longer be kept in separate watertight compartments, but are now having to learn to live side by side and this is forcing adherents of all faiths and none to ask questions that they have not asked before. Some members of all religions are frightened that contact with other religions will water down their own faith and way of life, and it is sad to see that there is still a small, though vocal, Christian group who feel that, even on such vital common matters as the care for the environment, it is more important to shout abuse at other faiths, than to work with them for 'one world'.

Also, then, on the agenda of many of the Church leaders is the question, 'How do we best relate to members of other faiths – in what regards are they our "allies" or our "enemies"?' It has to be remembered that the word Ecumenical which comes from the word *Oikumenia*, does not mean 'one Church' but 'one inhabited world'; what questions does that pose today when 'one inhabited world' can literally be on our own doorstep in our own street?

The House Churches

There has been a considerable haemorrhage suffered by the main Protestant Churches, and smaller losses by the Roman Catholic Church, to the so-called 'House Church Movement'. Everyone agrees that this is a far from satisfactory title for this new group but as yet there is no other generally accepted name:

> The phrase 'House Church Movement' has become one of those convenient labels that we stick on to a variety of Churches because they seem to be outside typical Christian experience. Unfortunately, convenient labels are difficult to remove once they become attached to anything; they become sanctioned by usage even if they are misleading in fact.

So writes Andrew Walker in his 1985 book *Restoring the Kingdom* (Hodder and Stoughton, page 17). But having written that, he still uses the title on his front page! He does suggest the title 'kingdom people', but this has not become accepted, and 'Restoration Churches' again does not meet with approval either within or outside the movement. In a real sense the word 'Independent' is historically and factually the easiest term to understand.

There are a number of different groupings or 'streams' within the movement, each with its own identifiable leaders. The links between individual Churches and streams is not easy to describe. Those inside the movement would argue that this is because the links are organic rather than organisational i.e. they depend on personal relationships between local Church leaders and leaders of their stream. At one extreme this is highly organised with the final say resting with the 'Apostolic Team'. At the other extreme some streams are more akin to a federation of largely autonomous Churches, but still with a clear sense of 'belonging'.

Independency has a long and honourable history in Church life, and there have always been groups who felt the institutional Churches were not for them. This new form of independency may have its roots in the Brethren, but its appearance in the sixties also came from the Charismatic Movement which has had its impact both inside and outside all denominations. It has brought a great deal of new life, new music and new joy into the lives of new and old Christians alike. As in the time of the Wesleys, the institutional Churches could not contain this new outpouring of the Spirit, so in the sixties and seventies it overflowed into many small independent groups:

> The years 1970–74 were heady days of great excitement and discovery; a discovery of meeting groups all over the country with similar beginnings and common aspirations. Those aspirations, on the whole, were related to 'walking with God' in such a way that the experiential and supernatural became a living grace that seemed to have done away with religious legalism once and for all. The legalism of clericalism, church order, standardised liturgies, denominational certainties, and dogmatic doctrines, were seen to be swept aside by the coming of the Spirit (Walker, op. cit., page 50).

Those who are caught up in such truly meaningful experiences rarely have time to read Church history and its record of religious enthusiasts and what happens to such movements. Today's liberation can become tomorrow's dogma. However our concern is with the effect of these new groups on the traditional Churches and what their future relationships should be. The evangelical wing of the Church of England was itself growing in influence and numbers, but also 'lost' many of its younger and more enthusiastic members to the House Churches. In most towns and cities such groups sprang up and came together for events like the Festival of Light, Bible Weeks, and other informal but often large gatherings.

In some places the new independent groups came about

by splits within a local Anglican, Baptist or Methodist Church, and a number of members followed a particular leader and set up a 'rival' group within the parish or area. In some the leader was ordained, but in others it was lay members who felt called to break away from established Churches. This was, and is, very painful, and the subsequent divisions created ran through families, as well as through Churches and parishes. In other cases small groups of individuals came together, started to worship in their own homes, but then outgrew the front room, and began to hire or eventually buy halls, cinemas and redundant churches, or built new ones for their growing congregations.

Relationships between these new independent groups and the institutional Churches were sometimes very bad, and there was real competition and rivalry, which did little good for the cause of Christ. By the time 'Not Strangers But Pilgrims' was launched things had begun to change a little. The new groups had begun to settle down and find themselves confronted with fresh divisions, but now within their own ranks and without any commonly accepted authority structure to help them.

In a semi-official response to the invitation to take part in the Inter-Church Process which was published in *Observations* (BCC, 1987) Philip Vogel wrote this about their attitudes towards relationships with the Churches:

> This would vary according to the different streams within the House Churches. One extreme would give a tacit recognition of the denominations but with very little practical involvement with these Churches. It would see such denominations as 'not being of God' and would see the future of the Church as outside the traditional denominations. The other extreme would be a recognition of God's Spirit working within the denominational Churches and a practical involvement and co-operation with them.

The House Churches did not feel able to take part in the Inter-Church Process, and stood apart from ecumenical involvement at national level. At local level there was co-operation in some places, and in Lent '86 replies came from some mixed groups with House Church folk in them, and also from some individual members of House Churches. However, significant and important conversations are now taking place between leaders of the House Churches and those in the Inter-Church Process, and organisations such as the Christian Enquiry Agency are building up practical working arrangements.

The denominations' loss of young people and able leaders to the House Churches frightened some local mainstream Churches into an even more traditional approach to life and worship. How were they to live with this seemingly new development?

It is hard to get exact statistics because there is no one overall body to represent the often kaleidoscopic nature of the internal relationships of the House Churches. Estimates vary between fifty and one hundred thousand. Such active groups of very committed Christians could not be ignored by the Inter-Church Process as it began its work.

In the face of these varied, but closely related, issues it needed great courage to start on the Inter-Church Process. After much prayer and heart-searching it was agreed that the pilgrimage must begin, but there were some who set out more in faith than in hope, and others who had very little of either.

3

A Voice from the Pews

On 7th May, 1985 at Lambeth Palace the leaders of thirty-two Churches in England, Scotland and Wales met formally and agreed to launch a 'three year Inter-Church Process of prayer, reflection and debate together on the nature and purpose of the Church in the light of its mission'. Later that year on the evening of November 8th, at St Peter's Church, Eaton Square, a ceremony was held to celebrate the launch, and representatives of the churches lit candles and placed them in a tray of earth. The candles burned side by side symbolising the undertaking given by those Churches to work alongside each other in this new initiative.

It was recognised that 'the prayer reflection and debate' must go on at all levels, and in the words of the Archbishop of Canterbury, 'Instead of hierarchies passing things down, this time we are trying it the right way – the local debate will be fed into the wider national reflection and discussion.' This was recognition that previous unity talks had tried things the other way round, and was in part the reason why they had failed.

The three years of the Process was to start with as wide a consultation as possible with grass-root members, and only then to be followed by a series of national conferences in 1987 leading finally to a British and Irish conference.

The preparatory work was divided into three sections and two Associate Secretaries were appointed to work with the Secretary of the Inter-Church Process Steering Group, the

Rev Colin Davey (BCC Secretary of the Division of Ecumenical Affairs).

Observations by Others

Colin Davey undertook the work of editing the section dealing with the many varied responses elicited from inside Britain, Ireland and beyond. He also fed into the Process the insights on the nature and purpose of the Church contained in the theological discussions including 'Baptism, Eucharist and Ministry'. He reported the views of local Christian communities and networks and those of the Aid Agencies, Theological Colleges and people in political and industrial life. One of the important preparatory conferences for this book was the one organised by the National Centre for Christian Communities and Networks (NACCCAN). Two themes that were often to be repeated in the Process find early and strong expression here: 'Lay people suffer. They love their church and want to remain within it but they find themselves driven into a wilderness with no way out. One of the problems is that little attention has been paid to a theology of the laity' (page 22). 'To bring Christianity alive means that individuals and the Church as a whole have to be willing to change. Some Churches are afraid of changing' (ibid., page 27).

After numerous other conferences and reports Colin Davey edited the book Observations on the Church from Britain and Abroad, which was one of the foundation documents for the Inter-Church Process. His was an attempt to see what the Church looked like to those who were either outside Britain, outside the participating Churches or on the fringe of the Church itself. As he wrote in the preface, 'The overall aim was that our picture of the nature and purpose of the Church should not be based only on self-portraits but also on a number of sketches which would show ourselves as others see us.' It was a disappointment that a number of groups invited to take part did not in fact do so and we were deprived of their help.

Self Reflections

Monsignor Vincent Nichols (General Secretary of the Roman Catholic Bishops' Conference of England and Wales) was one of the Associate Secretaries and he had the task of drawing together the official responses from the thirty-two Churches who had committed themselves to the Process. The question put to each was: 'In your tradition and experience, how do you understand the nature and purpose of your Church in relation to other Christian denominations as we share in God's mission to the world?' The actual responses vary in length and depth but all make interesting reading, and while some were the work of a commissioned individual, others represented hours of 'committee time' as Churches tried to express their own understanding of the nature of the Church. Each Church also gives brief outlines of its membership, ministers and buildings.

The responses were published under the title *Reflections: how Churches view their life and mission*. Vincent Nichols comments in his introduction, 'It is a unique collection; churches confessing to one another, in charity and honesty, their self-understanding and their reflections on their relationships with each other.'

The Local Voice

These were mainly the views of 'headquarters people', and if the Process was to get new insights into what people really felt at local level, another way had to be found to gather their views and present them to the conferences which were to follow as the final part of the Process.

When the Inter-Church Process was still being planned I had moved from being Archdeacon of Rochester and Secretary of the Kent Ecumenical Council, to become the Home Secretary of the Church of England's Board of Mission and Unity. I was given the particular brief to help encourage local ecumenism after the failure of the Covenant.

The Board then agreed that I could be seconded part-time to be the other Associate Secretary of the Inter-Church

Process with responsibility for gathering views of the local Churches and their members, and then to produce a companion book alongside *Observations* and *Reflections*. This was to be called *Views from the Pews* (British Council of Churches, 1986). But collecting the views of six million varied Christians throughout England, Scotland and Wales presented a big challenge and there were times when I envied my two colleagues their important but more limited task!

Twenty years earlier, the British Council of Churches had arranged an ambitious course called 'People Next Door', and this was the first time that a nationally organised ecumenical course had been arranged. We had used it on our Bristol housing estate, and the impact it made on the members of our three different Churches meeting together in a number of people's front rooms, had been considerable. Twenty years on, the initials 'PND' still had local meaning in many places, and some groups were still meeting who traced their ecumenical roots back to this course which had encouraged Church people to meet together, and then look beyond their Church boundaries. The PND experience was one of the main models for the 1986 course 'What on Earth is the Church For?' or Lent '86 as it is usually known.

Local Radio

How could we reach the people out there in their separate Churches and fellowships, and equally important, how could they share with us their real feelings? PND involved about seventy thousand people in many groups and used study material and tapes produced by the British Council of Churches. Since then a new means of communication had become widely available, and had been much welcomed by some people in the Churches – namely local radio. There was also an organisation, The Churches' Advisory Council for Local Broadcasting (CACLB), and its linked Association of Christians in Local Broadcasting (ACLB), which not only brought together all Christians working in local radio, but even more surprisingly spanned the BBC and the Independent Local Radio (ILR) divide!

In 1986 the BBC had twenty-eight local stations in England, with national stations for Wales and Scotland and there was a growing number of Independent Local Radio stations throughout Britain. They brought a new style of broadcasting to the country, and their informality and local flavour made them excellent vehicles for the expression of community feelings and views. In some places the Churches had invested people and substantial funding into local radio. But most local stations relied largely on volunteers, drawn from all Christian traditions, who devoted time and skill to presenting the Christian message and local Church news to their own locality.

There are a number of claims by BBC stations as to who put out the first 'Radio Lent Course', and it is likely that it was one of the Midland stations that did so in the early seventies. Certainly when I went to Kent in 1976 the idea was well established, and BBC Radio Medway (now BBC Radio Kent), was very willing to work with the Churches in promoting a Lent course. What the Churches of Kent were able to add to what had been done elsewhere was joint promotion and planning of the Lent course in full co-operation with the local station. Over the years the Radio Kent Lent Course built up a considerable listening and responding audience, and on some Tuesday evenings there were nearly a hundred thousand people taking part in Kent, South London and Essex where the station could be heard.

The courses brought together hundreds of small groups in almost every town and village. They met in people's homes and were mainly led by lay men and women rather than the clergy and ministers. Even the smallest group in the most remote part of the county could have Delia Smith, Malcolm Muggeridge, Sheila Cassidy, Terry Waite or Mary O'Hara in their front room, and after a discussion period, a chance to put their questions direct to the speaker in the studio by telephone.

It was this experience (shared elsewhere as well) which encouraged us to explore the possibility of a Lent course organised nationally, but carried out by as many local radio stations as possible. Well before the Lambeth Palace launch of 'Not Strangers But Pilgrims', a group drawn from the Churches and local radio stations had begun exploring the idea, as we knew that such a completely new concept of Church communication could not be achieved overnight. There were many who doubted, and sadly some who opposed. The whole scheme was very nearly stillborn at the end of 1984 when a fairly senior official in BBC local radio decreed that, if ILR stations were taking part, the BBC ones could not, and issued instructions accordingly. Fortunately the Churches had put sufficient resources into local radio and enough Christians were working in local stations (both BBC and ILR) to get the decision reversed.

However, by dint of much travelling, talking, praying and persuading, Lent '86 went out on fifty-seven different stations and reached an astonishing one million people. The BBC and ILR stations in Ireland (North and South) who were more than willing to carry the course, could not do so without the full backing of the Irish Churches, and this was not obtained. Almost every BBC station put out a course, as did many ILR stations; Radio Scotland had a national course which was used throughout Scotland with considerable effect, and Wales had programmes in both English and Welsh. A course was also broadcast on Forces Radio in Germany and Holland and in the Far East. The involvement of all three of the Armed Services was a major factor in Lent '86, and it was a nice touch that the very first response we received was from a Royal Navy ship on its way back from the Falklands, who did the 'Lent' course three months ahead of anyone else!

What on Earth is the Church For?

The basis of the many different programmes put out by the stations, and of the cassette course which we also produced, was the best-selling book *What on Earth is the Church For?* written by Canon Martin Reardon. This was intended mainly as a guide for leaders and speakers, but in fact sold

120,000 copies in a few weeks, and played a major part in this time of preparation.

It was illustrated with photos and cartoons and proved an invaluable resource alongside the radio programmes and the cassette course, and in fact some groups used only this book as the basis of their groups. It was divided into five chapters so providing a section for each week, and ended with general questions for the group to discuss. At the last moment we also produced a book for youth groups called *Whose Church is it Anyway?*

It was decided that there must be a mechanism to elicit response from the groups and individuals taking part, so there would be clear statistical evidence to put before the Churches about the feelings of local Christians. The course was therefore planned to provide an opportunity for groups to reply through their leader and/or send individual views as they wished. Each copy of the book contained a section made up of response sheets, and these were also available as separate leaflets. A quarter of a million of these were sold and circulated. It is worth recording that, thanks to the co-operation of Churches, radio stations, the Jerusalem Trust and the Hockerill Education Foundation, the total cost to the Churches themselves was under fifteen thousand pounds for the whole of this great and unique exercise.

The course dealt with the questions of ecumenism, but also followed the request of the Roman Catholic Church and others, to focus on questions dealing with the nature of the Church itself. It was designed to explore people's beliefs about the nature and purpose of the Church, their understanding of the life of Christ and how that life could be expressed today in their local Church. The five weekly titles were:

Why believe in God?
What did Jesus come for?
Why did the Church begin?
Why different Churches?
What now?

As the weeks went by it was clear that the course had been taken up very widely indeed and that the local Councils of Churches (often working closely with the local radio station) were mainly responsible for the success of the groups. Of course not everyone took part and others would only do the course in the security of their own denominational groups. This was a pity because so much of the value lay in the local groups being as diverse in their membership as possible and the same applied to the programmes themselves. It was also regrettable, though perhaps understandable, that some clergy and ministers could not trust the groups to meet without them, and not a few group replies included such phrases as 'We had an excellent discussion until the vicar came in', a comment echoed in Scotland but substituting 'the minister'!

The Response

There were just three weeks between the last Lenten broadcast and April 12th, which was the date given for all replies to be sent back either via the radio stations, or directly to Church House, Westminster, where I had my office.

The response was completely overwhelming and far exceeded our wildest hopes both in quantity and quality. I am not sure if we established a record for the largest amount of post ever received in two weeks at Church House, but the daily pile of GPO sacks was quite astounding and very exciting. Fortunately it was half term and all our schoolchildren were brought in to open sacks and sort out forms! A formerly rather dismissive Religious Correspondent of *The Times* was converted to the Process by the sight of the volume of replies, and the quality of the few hundred he had time to glance at in my office.

Because of the deadline we were never able to assess everything that came in, and replies continued to pour in over the next months, but Trumedia Study Oxford Ltd used a percentage sample of about ten thousand individual replies and a few hundred of the group replies carefully selected from the eighteen regions that processed them. As Judy

Turner Smith (the researcher of Trumedia and author of the report) wrote in the preface to *Views from the Pews*:

> It is likely that more than a million people took part and that the opinions of more than just those who sent in their questionnaires have been gathered through the group reports. It must however be pointed out that the results from Lent '86, however valuable in themselves, cannot be said to represent the views of Church-goers in Britain; what we do have is a fair idea of the views of those who responded. That was however over 100,000 ordinary people, the largest cross section yet available, so their voice deserves to be heard (*Views from the Pews op. cit.*, page 3).

In addition to all this personal material, and to separate reports on Wales and Scotland, another important section of local responses came from Sponsoring Bodies, Councils of Churches and the growing number of Local Ecumenical Projects. The Rev Hugh Cross (the BCC Ecumenical Officer for England) quickly wrote up their insights and feelings and added them to *Views from the Pews*. Here were more strong local voices demanding to be heard.

The report had to be written at tremendous speed so that it could be published in the early autumn of 1986; and another group worked on a video which showed both what had happened in Lent '86, and what were the main findings from it. This also came out in the autumn, but was not seen by as many of the Lent '86 groups as we had hoped.

Local Views

Views from the Pews still rewards study (as does all the original material which is stored in hundreds of boxes in the archives of Nottingham University Library). Here we can only draw out the main 'headline conclusions' and then look at some of the main issues relevant to the growth of local ecumenism. On page 43 they are summarised under five headings, and here I give them with a single group report 'quote' to give the flavour of the findings which were to play such an important part in all that followed:

1. *Grass-roots find a voice* 'As our fellowship grew and openness to each other's differences emerged, we became more aware of our ignorance of each other's beliefs and practices. We also believe that this growing together is still being frustrated by ecclesiastical barriers from the top.' (Group in Scotland)

2. *Jesus hidden by jargon* 'The language of worship was not good for people today in describing Jesus. Justifier meant nothing. Redeemer − very little, except to older people who remembered the pawn shops.' (Group in Yorkshire)

3. *Afraid to share* 'We often know what we believe but so often we lack the words and the courage to share it with others; we need more help in simple ways of sharing our faith in informal ways.' (Group in Hampshire)

4. *Enjoying our differences* 'Everyone in the group thought that the differences between our Churches were blown up out of all proportion, and diversity is a good thing; in fact it was likened to a bunch of flowers.' (Group in Southern England)

5. *Time to be one* 'Although denominational differences probably serve a useful purpose in adding colour and variety in the Church, they should not be seen as insurmountable barriers to greater unified activity. The view was expressed that theologians may get in the way of Christian unity and may be doing the ''Church corporate'' a dis-service. True unity would probably arise from the grass-roots rather than be imposed from above.' (Basingstoke)

These views occur again and again in the replies from individuals and groups. There were differences of emphasis from place to place, and from denomination to denomination, and also from differing age groups, but the overall impression from this great mountain of paper was of a remarkably unified response roughly summarised under these headings and in the single realisation that *to be different is not to be wrong.* Until now people felt that they must defend their differences from other Christians, but having met and talked and prayed together they wanted to share their differences without either being ashamed of them or feeling they must impose them on others.

We asked people to identify themselves by age and denomination, but it is remarkable how little these factors seem to have affected their replies when their views had been forged together in small ecumenical groups, and not in denominational isolation.

Two other matters from the replies are also relevant to the theme of this book. On the third week, members were given nine different phrases to choose from to best express their understanding of the word 'Church'. An astonishing eighty-three per cent chose the phrase, 'The body of all Christians, past, present and to come.' This was clear favourite over such definitions as 'the denomination' or 'the Diocese' or 'the local building'. It is interesting that the definition which came second was 'the local congregation or assembly of Christians'. Those who took part in Lent '86 were clear that the word Church means people and not just structures.

The other matter is that of reception of Communion in each other's Churches:

The most frequent specific concern is the strong desire for joint Holy Communion. Sometimes it may have been true that those contributing such remarks were unaware of the difficulties which have prevented this in the past, but a remarkable number were aware. This does not seem to have inhibited the desire for joint Communion but rather to have increased the pain at its absence. It did not seem appropriate to respondents that such an expression of oneness in Christ should have to wait until formal unity might be achieved and in the words of an East Midlands group, 'We think Christ must wring his hands in anguish at the way we have allowed the Eucharist, Mass or Communion to become such a divisive exercise – who can and who can't; who may and who must. Shame on us! (*Views from the Pews, op. cit.*, page 33)

Local Experience

Some of this is not pleasant reading for the Churches, and
it is not surprising that *Views from the Pews* was banned from
some Church bookshops and stalls as there was too much
strong meat in it. It is true (as Judy Turner Smith pointed
out), that these are only the views of those who were
prepared to come and take part in the groups, and then
write in and express themselves. Many more would do none
of these things, and they are also part of the Church. But
no longer can Church leaders shelter behind the view, 'Oh,
my people would not wear that idea.' 'My people' are
prepared to wear a lot and feel that their views have not
been wanted or listened to.

  Not everyone is prepared to pick up his or her pack and
become a pilgrim for unity, but there is a large company
who are, and many of them are impatient with the church
hierarchies. There is a strong feeling that it is the clergy who
are the 'stopper in the bottle'. A group from the Channel
Islands spoke for many, 'It was felt strongly that the laity
are far more ready to accept unity which would probably
be much further ahead, except for Church leaders and the
so-called cleverness of theologians.'

  The strength of these individual views is underlined by
the second section of *Views from the Pews*: the views from
existing ecumenical councils and Local Ecumenical Projects.
'If we had waited until we completely understood and
agreed with each other we would never have got anywhere.
It is through common action that we have found our way
towards common understanding' (Abingdon Council of
Churches).

  Looking at the mass of information prepared in these three
publications (*Reflections*; *Observations*; and *Views from the
Pews*) for the 1987 round of conferences, there are clear
pointers to the next steps. At all levels friendship and
openness are starting to replace fear and suspicion, and this
is just as true of the much maligned Church leaders and
theologians, as it is of the house group in the front room.
It is also clear that the way forward in unity is not to be

restricted to bilateral talks between Churches, but a much wider approach seeking to draw together all the strands of Christian worship, organisation and experience, to be expressed in practical terms and ways.

Previous schemes failed because Churches and individuals felt threatened, and feared they would lose their own ethos and identity. This came out very clearly from the Lent '86 replies. People valued their own Churches and ways of doing things; they did not want a uniformity; they 'rejoiced in their differences', but did not see that this prevented them from sharing with others and in return gaining new insights and visions.

In the past unity had been seen as a threat; now perhaps it could be seen as a blessing and an opportunity. In part this has happened because we are now in a mission situation in the United Kingdom, surrounded by people of other faiths and of none. We are therefore better able to see how much we have in common with our fellow Christians, whom we no longer see as opponents. In Lent '86, and in a growing number of places and conferences at all levels, people were astonished to find that most of their perceptions about other Christians were not based on current reality. Once they had met as fellow Christians the religious labels that they wore on Sundays seemed insignificant in the light of what they had shared with each other.

'Knowledge of each other's traditions proved not only inadequate but even grossly inaccurate, having been based on rumour rather than fact. For many, this discovery of more accurate information and common ground, quite apart from any other result from the Lent '86 course, was encouraging, even liberating' (*Views from the Pews, op. cit.*, page 32).

At the end of 1986 large packets of books and papers began to drop through the letter boxes of many hundreds of people in England, Scotland and Wales. These were people chosen by their Churches to come together, first to the English, Welsh or Scottish Conferences, as appropriate, and then in the British Conference at Swanwick in Derbyshire in September 1987.

Whatever lay in the future for the Churches at the national

level, one woman in the North-East of England had no doubt what must happen in her village, 'I feel that Lent '86 has opened a door leading to a new concept of our brothers and sisters in Christ. I feel it is our responsibility, in this village, to keep that door ever open, and if possible, to remove it from its hinges, and lose it.'

4

Eucharist and Euphoria

However much London and the South-East may think they are the centre of England (not to say of Britain!), there can be no doubt that the ecumenical centre lies in the East Midlands. The Hayes Conference Centre at Swanwick in central Derbyshire has hosted many meetings of the British Council of Churches' Assembly in the past, and was the natural venue for the climax of the Inter-Church Process in September 1987. In March, Nottingham University, only a few miles away, housed the National Conference for England.

The Four Nations

Over the years one of the biggest challenges that the British Council of Churches has had to live with is that of the four nations living within these islands. England, Scotland, Wales and Ireland have a great deal in common, especially in Church life, but they also have a considerable national diversity. Because of this the Irish, the Scottish and the Welsh have developed their own distinctive national Councils of Churches to reflect their own scene. These worked very closely with the British Council, but they kept asking, 'Where is the *English* Council of Churches?' There wasn't one.

Though this may seem understandable to the English, who thought they made up such a large part of the BCC that they sometimes forgot those who came from the Celtic fringes (or heartland depending on your point of view), it was, needless to say, a cause of continuing concern and some friction to the others.

In the seventies and early eighties, the English local ecumenical scene began to outstrip that of the other three nations. LEPs were virtually unknown outside England, and local Councils of Churches, though growing in number, were not so common. The setting up in 1974 of the Consultative Committee for Local Ecumenical Projects in England (CCLEPE) went some way to giving England its own specialist ecumenical body; but this body, while being significant in having the Roman Catholic Church as a full and active member from the beginning, only dealt with a very limited field of work and had no full-time staff of its own.

One of the many questions facing the Churches in the new Process was how the Churches of the four nations could best work together at the level of Britain and Ireland, and where it would be better if matters were dealt with in separate national bodies – assuming it was agreed that under any new arrangement England should have its own national body.

The affirmation of both the national and the British and Irish relationship underlay the planning of the 1987 series of conferences. They must begin in England, Wales and Scotland, and then progress to a final one for Britain as a whole. As there was not to be an Irish conference, the Irish Churches would be invited to send observers to all three national conferences and to the final Swanwick gathering.

The preparatory material described at the end of chapter three was common to all, and each national conference was organised by its own preparatory working party. This worked well with each of them being distinctive of its own unique nationality. The small Steering Group of twenty had the marathon opportunity of attending all three conferences within a period of ten days! We went as observers, and not as a central organising committee, though most of us were intimately involved with the preparations for one of the three.

Those attending the conferences were appointed by the Churches who were asked to make them as widely representative as possible. In the case of the large Churches (the Church of England with a team of 135 at Nottingham and the Roman Catholics with 90) it was relatively easy to get a balance of male and female, young and old, black and white, lay and ordained, 'top brass' and 'grass-roots'. It was much more difficult for a small Church with just two delegates! The Churches were especially asked to ensure that those whom they appointed were not all ecumenical enthusiasts, but included some who were at the most 'luke warm'. If the delegates were to represent their Churches and then report back to them, they must reflect the whole range of feelings, or there would be no hope of carrying their denomination forward into the next step of the Process.

Nottingham

England held the first conference, and on the evening of Friday March 27th 1987 the University Campus at Nottingham was buzzing with the arrival of four hundred people. As they arrived (through a most violent storm) it was obvious that this was going to be a conference with a difference: seventeen Roman Catholic bishops, fifteen Anglican ones and URC moderators and Methodist Chairmen two-a-penny; but alongside these dignitaries were many who had never been to a residential gathering before and some of them, while conscious of the honour and opportunity offered to them, were unsure of their standing. Black Christians were well represented both within traditional denominations, and in the new black-led Churches themselves. Though there was a good gathering of grey-haired and bald, there were also younger people and the Methodist and United Reformed Church groups brought the average down a bit. Every Church in England, except for the Russian and Greek Orthodox whose members at the last moment were unable to be there, was represented.

The Conference Planning Group had decided that the

forty-eight hour conference must begin where Lent '86 had
left off – namely in small groups. Imagine the chaos of
directing four hundred people into thirty-four different
groups in a strange building that very few people even
knew. However, it worked, and suddenly a housewife from
Newcastle or a chemist from Truro found they had in their
group the Archbishop of Liverpool, or the Bishop of Bristol
plus a varied assortment of 'strangers' from every part of
the country. The first group sessions concentrated on
meeting and talking, and even more importantly listening
and learning. All had received the three preparatory books
and a list of questions arising from them. The main question
was how could they now progress towards a closer working
together, while at the same time hold dear and precious their
own denominational experiences and treasures?

This part of the conference worked well, and at the end
of the first twenty-four hours most people seemed to be
relating, and the hum of conversation at meals and in the
groups indicated that the planning was bearing fruit.
Informal black-led worship on Saturday morning banished
any hesitation and coolness that might still be felt.

However, later on the Saturday we hit a problem.

There was sadness and some anger about the practical
arrangements for the Roman Catholic Mass that evening.
Planning the worship for the conference was one of the
biggest problems for the Planning Group. After much heart-
searching it had been agreed that there should be worship
led by each of the main traditions, and that this should
include Eucharistic celebrations. The Roman Catholic Mass
was planned for Saturday evening, with a final Anglican
Communion at the end of Sunday afternoon. But it was
known that the issue of Eucharistic services, at which not
everyone present would be able to communicate, would be
very painful. This had been brought out by the strength of
feeling from the Lent Groups on just this point.

In order to go some way to meet this feeling it was agreed
that when the Archbishop of Liverpool, the Rt Rev Derek
Worlock, celebrated Mass, he would invite non-Catholics
to come forward with the Catholics to receive a blessing.

Unfortunately when the order of service was printed this invitation was omitted, and instead there was the request that non-Catholics should remain in their places. Despite a most helpful address by the Archbishop some were still left with much heart-searching and sorrow.

As a result, on the following day, Sunday, after a calmly inspirational preaching service led by the Rev Kathleen Richardson (Chairman of the West Yorkshire Methodist District) feelings still ran high and there was a difficult plenary session and strong words were used. It is breaking no confidences to say that at lunch-time it looked possible that the Roman Catholic bishops might withdraw from the conference and from the Inter-Church Process itself. For some it was their first experience of the somewhat freer atmosphere of Christian debate in ecumenical gatherings that others had grown used to over the years, but others again felt that the debate was insensitive and even arrogant and a 'power play' by a few.

But thanks to some 'holy oil' poured on the situation, the conference went forward and, despite a rather crucial photo-copier breakdown in the last session, an agreed report and statement was accepted. There was agreement that new ways of working at all levels in England and in Britain and Ireland must be found, and a number of important recommendations to go forward to the Swanwick Conference were agreed.

The final act of Eucharistic worship was led by the Chairman of the Inter-Church Process, the Archbishop of York, Dr John Habgood. At the Communion few if any people remained in their seats, and there were emotional moments as Catholic, Anglican, Baptist, Salvationist and Quaker, went forward together. As yet, not all could or would, receive the sacrament of Christ's presence, but we were there together sharing in our pain and our joy, and no one could feel that he or she was merely a spectator.

Bangor

If you want to go to Bangor by train it is not a good idea to start from Nottingham! However the Steering Group got there and settled into the more relaxed atmosphere of a small North Wales University College. The Welsh conference, organised by the Council of Churches for Wales, was the smallest of the three, with 150 members, and lasted from lunch-time on Tuesday March 31st, till lunch on Thursday April 2nd.

It was a different world from Nottingham and there was a strong emphasis on Welsh consciousness and culture. We loved the singing, but found the two languages one more barrier, when denominations already divided by theology, were also subdivided again by language.

However, it was noticeable that although translation facilities were available, most speakers used English in the sessions so the visitors did not feel left out. Many of the same issues as had surfaced at Nottingham were voiced here, but there was not the same strong lay voice, nor were there as many people present who had taken part in the Lent course. In part this was because the conference took place mid-week and not at a weekend as in England and Scotland.

Small groups were again used as the basis of the conference but there was no great crisis over worship. The fact that in Wales some of the main Churches had already entered into a National Covenant, and that there existed an agreed ecumenical Eucharist, was a positive plus on the Welsh scene. However, one still felt the lack of ecumenical experience at the local level. As reported by the Rev Noel Davies in *Views from the Pews* (*Views from the Pews, op. cit.*) out of the ninety known Councils only ten responded to a questionnaire on their activities: 'More than eighty per cent were in urban areas and most in predominantly English speaking rather than Welsh speaking communities' (page 9). Moreover there was a strong representation of Independency in Wales, and this added a dimension largely missing in England and Scotland.

I had the good fortune to be attached to one of the small groups which had an Irish observer in it, and learnt a good deal about the Irish scene as we discussed the Welsh! There was already some sadness that Ireland was not more fully involved in the Inter-Church Process and it was recognised that whatever happened in Britain must have some effect on Ireland as well. But there was more taking place in both the North and South of Ireland than might be realised from the papers or news-bulletins, and the Ballymascanlon Inter Church Meetings were an ongoing commitment with permanent working departments on theological and social issues funded by the Churches.

A unanimous conference report was arrived at, which would clearly lead to a strengthening of the work of the Council of Churches for Wales and also the Covenanted Churches, with more effective machinery for encouraging unity at both the regional and local levels, and there seemed to be no great conflict in a revised and renewed Welsh body working alongside, and with, an overall British and Irish body as well. There was also a call for a greater place for a gathering of young people in Wales, and the part that they could play in getting ecumenical matters under way at the local level.

St Andrews

Friday morning had the Steering Group studying more train timetables, as we set off on another cross-country rail journey which eventually took us to Edinburgh, and then on to the ancient University and golfing 'mecca' of St Andrews.

The change of temperature and mood was considerable and we knew we were in Scotland. We were especially glad that the Chairman of the Steering Group was Bishop Alastair Haggart, the recently retired Primus of the Episcopal Church in Scotland. He was able to alert those of us who have lived most of our lives south of Hadrian's Wall, as to what to expect! Whereas in England and Wales the media interest in our conferences was negligible, at St Andrews it was intense, and TV, Radio, and the Press were on hand most of the time – as was the opposition. The hall of residence where we stayed was picketed by the very vocal and aggressive supporters of Jack Glass, who waved

banners at us as we went in and out. We were informed
that we were consorting with the Evil One because we had
Roman Catholics meeting with us. I saw a young Salvation
Army officer in uniform being physically threatened by such
a group, but perhaps it was good for us to be reminded that
there are still those who think of ecumenism as an
opportunity for confrontation rather than co-operation.

I found the St Andrews conference fascinating, but I was
aware that I was in a different world as well as a different
country. Here religion was taken very seriously as the media
interest showed, and religion was a matter of theology, and
right theology at that. There were 210 gathered there, and
they represented every aspect of Scottish Church life which,
in the past, had been even more polarised than in England
or Wales. But there were signs of hope, and despite the
banner-wavers on the doorstep, the fact that the Roman
Catholic Church in Scotland representatives, led by Bishop
Conti, were there and taking an active part, was a major
advance in itself. Of course the large Church of Scotland
delegation of seventy people dominated some aspects of
the conference, and as the largest and the established
Church in Scotland, this was only to be expected.

Scotland also had the advantage of having on hand the
results of Lent '87. The impact of Lent '86 was probably
greater in proportion in Scotland than anywhere else in
Britain, and they decided to build on this and plan a Scottish
Lent course for 1987 as well. As Lent was drawing to its
close during the conference, the views of the many groups
were fed directly into us. The local lay voice was therefore
of considerable importance and was listened to.

The Scottish Churches Council already played an
important part in the life of many Churches, and Scotland
was small enough to have a 'family feeling' about its
relationships, but big enough to keep the rest of Britain
firmly in our place! The most lively issue at St Andrews was
not the role of the Scottish Council, but what its relationship
should be, if any, with the rest of Britain. Some wondered
if there needed to be any 'British' body in addition to a
Council for each of the four nations. Although in the end

the majority feeling was that there should be two levels, it was most important that those of us from outside Scotland should hear and recognise this authentic Scottish note.

Preparing for Swanwick

This was my strongest memory as we withdrew late on the Sunday night and headed for Edinburgh airport and a quick flight back to London. In ten days our small group had had the unique privilege of meeting and being part of the three most representative gatherings of Christians ever to meet in England, Wales and Scotland. We had learnt much and experienced even more, and somehow we had to shape all this joy and tension into the preparations for the final Swanwick gathering which was just five months away.

The key questions were still the same as before; 'the nature and purpose of the Church in the light of its mission to the world' or 'What on Earth is the Church For?' But now our clearer theological understanding must find expression in some new form of inter-Church co-operation which should in no way replace the Churches, but be the servant of the Churches working as one.

Much had been learnt from the three conferences, and from the many years of experience in the British, and other Councils of Churches; but it still had to be seen whether the British Churches would support the new moves, and in particular if the Roman Catholic Church would continue its commitment beyond the Inter-Church Process into future plans and throw its considerable influence behind them. We needed, too, to know that what emerged would be helpful in the Irish situation.

A new phrase was beginning to be used, and often disliked and misunderstood: 'ecumenical instruments'. There was a feeling that the age of 'Councils' was passing, and we had to find a new method and a new terminology to express the way in which separated Churches, still with profound differences in worship and practice, could none-the-less show oneness in mission and proclamation of the Gospel. 'Instruments' may be blunt or sharp, they can also perform a variety of tasks such as digging-over a weed patch, and in the right hands can play inspiring music, or perform miracles by delicate surgical operations.

When the Steering Group next met together these were the main issues confronting us and also the Church leaders in the Inter-Church Meeting to whom we reported. We all felt encouraged, but somewhat daunted especially as we had such a short time to get the final conference ready. The biggest single anxiety was again worship, and it is worth noting that it was by a single vote that we held to our decision to ask each nation and denomination to offer worship in their own style and tradition, and not just have 'ecumenical worship'. Looking back this may have been the most important decision we made, and it was backed up by the Church leaders we consulted. It is also important to note that the pattern and place of worship was planned first, and the rest of the conference then placed around it.

The Swanwick conference was planned for 320 participants, and this included twenty young stewards drawn equally from all four nations. Their lively and somewhat rebellious presence set the tone from the start. They had been meeting in prayer before we arrived and had devised the opening worship which, with some humour, encouraged us to 'travel light' and decide what were to be our real priorities in the next few days.

It was agreed that, apart from the stewards, the various Church delegations should, if possible, have two-thirds of their membership from those who had been at the national conferences, but that there should be a somewhat higher Church-leadership element for this final five-day British conference. This meant that the Cardinal Archbishop of Westminster, the Archbishop of Canterbury, the President of the Methodist Conference and the Moderator of the General Assembly of the Church of Scotland, and other important leaders of their denominations were all participants, and were present for the whole of the conference.

But the delegations were again almost all chosen by their Churches and not by ecumenical groupings – a fact which caused some sorrow in ecumenical circles. Most delegations were large enough to include a number of lay people who continued to represent 'the group in the front room' from Lent '86. They were beginning to realise that their 'views from the pews' were being heard, and that they should keep on giving them to all who would listen. But whether there would be an adequate lay voice in the structures which finally emerged from all this talk was of great concern to them, and still continues as a very live issue.

An Historic Five Days

The Hayes Conference Centre in the small town of Swanwick, in Derbyshire, is probably the best known conference centre for all Christians in Britain, and this extraordinary Swanwick Centre has played host to many famous gatherings since its inception in 1920. In 1950 I first attended 'Study Swanwick' organised by the Student Christian Movement, which itself has played such a big part in training people in ecumenical matters.

But in 1987, from Bank Holiday Monday, August 31st, to Friday September 4th, it became the focus for evaluating the whole of the three year Inter-Church Process 'Not Strangers But Pilgrims', and for discovering the way forward for Churches together in Britain and Ireland.

Although most of those who had come had already played an active part in the preliminary stages of this Process, there was still great uncertainty as to what this gathering might achieve. Not one word of the final document was written until well into the conference itself, and some of it was still being written as the final lunch was served. A lot of hopes had been raised, but there was also a lot of disillusionment from past conferences which had talked much but seemed to have achieved very little. Because of the success of the small groups in Lent '86 and at the national conferences, the whole of the first two days, apart from worship, was spent in small groups and even the most senior Church leaders present were 'encouraged' to take part in all the small group meetings, and not hive off into other, perhaps more familiar or congenial, gatherings. In these groups the theological and practical questions already familiar from earlier part of the Inter-Church Process, were again debated but with a new urgency knowing that the time for decisions was on hand.

It was my task beforehand to allocate people into these groups, and with the help of my son and his computer, we tackled the task of creating thirty groups of twelve, wherein every group should ideally have: eight English, three Scots, one and a half Welsh, and about a quarter of an Irish person. It should also have at least three young people, one black person and eight men and four women. Then add into the equation that each group must have three senior clerics and at least four lay people; stir and make certain that all the major Churches have a representative in each group and that there is at least one voice that can speak for the smaller Churches! The computer got red hot, but somehow out of it emerged fascinating groups where, once again, the lay and local voice was heard and listened to across national and denominational divides. Several of the Church leaders, including Cardinal Hume himself, agreed that it was this experience of time spent together talking, meeting and praying as a small group, that convinced them that, despite all the difficulties, they were no longer strangers but fellow pilgrims.

The other 'converting factor' was the worship, and it is agreed that this played a vital part. We learnt from the mistakes at Nottingham, and at the first of the daily Eucharists, which was again the Roman Catholic Mass, the careful and loving presentation by the Cardinal and the invitation he gave for everyone to come forward at the Communion, made it one of the great ecumenical turning points. Because this is now becoming the norm it is worth actually quoting the words printed in the order of service: 'When Holy Communion is distributed, members of other denominations are warmly invited to come forward, if they wish, to one of the priests to receive a blessing as a sign of our real but, as yet, incomplete unity.' As Alastair Haggart writes in the preface to the Swanwick Report, 'Each tradition was loyal to its own present disciplines, so that there could be no general eucharistic hospitality, but many who could not receive the sacrament came forward for a blessing. Written and then read, that may appear nothing; experienced it was profound.'

The second Eucharist was that of the Covenanted Churches of Wales, and the joy here was to see the Roman Catholics, who had so lovingly shared the Peace and Blessings at their Mass, themselves come forward to receive blessing at the hands of the Welsh clergy and ministers, including a woman minister. To my knowledge every Roman Catholic present came forward and received a blessing in word, if not in sacrament. It fell to a surprised Welsh United Reformed minister to personally bless a Cardinal, at what was agreed to be a truly wonderful and symbolic service.

The final Eucharist offered by the Church of Scotland was also very meaningful, but was administered in our seats, so did not have quite the same visual impact as the other two. But those who, because of their own Church discipline, could not take bread or wine found themselves handing the paten and the cup to their neighbour, so serving them at the Lord's Supper.

More than any other action in that remarkable week these three shared Communion services are remembered and talked about.

One non-eucharistic service which was immensely significant was called 'The Healing of Ecumenical Memories' and the Rt Rev Graham Chadwick, Bishop of St Asaph, led us deep into our emotional and spiritual depths to lay bare and then be healed of the hurts received from, and resentment felt against, other Churches and Christians. To quote Alastair Haggart again: 'Unity comes as a gift and the gift − imperfect as yet, but profoundly real − was given and received in chapel.'

By the Wednesday evening the conference began to develop its own internal and probably inevitable crises; people were growing and learning through the groups and through the daily worship, but they were afraid that there was only a day and a half left and we did not seem to be getting anywhere. But we were.

On the Thursday, for the first time, denominational and national groups met separately to see where they thought we had got to, and the results of these meetings proved crucial at the afternoon plenary session which followed these lunch-time gatherings all over the conference site.

Conference goers will know that early afternoon plenary sessions are the most difficult to run, and even at the best conferences a degree of somnolence can descend. There was an element of this on that afternoon until the session Chairman the Rev Bernard Thorogood (the General Secretary of the United Reformed Church) noticed that Cardinal Hume, sitting at the back of the hall, had indicated he would like to speak.

Speaking from a few notes, he then held everyone spellbound as very simply but with complete clarity, he renewed the Roman Catholic Church's commitment to full engagement in the Inter-Church Process and to what could come out of it. 'I hope that our Roman Catholic delegates . . . will recommend to members of our Church that we move now quite deliberately from a situation of co-operation to one of commitment to each other.'

Knowing that he had arrived on the Monday uncertain as to what lead he should give, the clarity and power of his words were quite overwhelming. He seemed to catch the mood of everyone in the hall and raise expectations to new levels. It was an astonishing moment which no one present in the hall will forget. He went on: 'This commitment, then, should be official policy at every level. But we should have in view a moving, in God's time, to full communion, or communion that is both visible and organic . . . In full communion we recognise, of course, that there will not be uniformity but legitimate diversity. It is not often stressed sufficiently that even within the Roman Catholic Church there is considerable diversity.'

He then ended with these words. 'Christian unity is a gift from God and in these last few days I have felt He has been giving us this gift in abundance. It is also a process of growth. I would distrust anybody who tries to indicate to me what the end of that process will be. One step at a time, and Swanwick has been a very decisive one.'

The reception given to this speech was immediate and deeply moving, and I had the joy of being on the platform, and so able to see the unashamed emotional tears of many in the hall. The overworked word 'historic' must be used of that afternoon. Few had expected such a clear and unambiguous statement, but it came in part as a result of his meeting at lunch-time with the Roman Catholic delegates at the conference, from England, Wales and Scotland.

The Archbishop of Canterbury spoke through the waves of applause and, on behalf of the Church of England present, rejoiced at this statement, and pledged the same full support. Then in quick succession, the leaders of the Church of Scotland and of the other denominations in the three nations joined the welcome given by Dr Robert Runcie. It is important to record this, as the reception by such diverse and, in the past, such totally opposed Churches is as important as Cardinal Hume's statement itself.

The Swanwick Declaration

The whole atmosphere had changed and it was clear that the conference was ready, willing, and felt able to affirm a new move forward into commitment. The days of co-operation were passing, and the day of common commitment could begin. In recognition of the part that the local Christians had played in helping make this movement possible, it was agreed that an immediate Swanwick Declaration be issued from the Conference to be read in every Church in Britain as soon as possible. The midnight oil was burnt and the Declaration was typed and re-typed many times until in the dying moments of the conference, as we received our pilgrim shells at the chapel door, the final version was agreed and personally signed by almost every member still present.

At the heart of the Swanwick Declaration there stand these words which were forged first in thousands of house groups, Councils of Churches and Local Ecumenical Projects, refined at many conferences and then finally shaped by the Cardinal, Archbishop and the Swanwick Conference:

> It is our conviction that, as a matter of policy at all levels and in all places, our Churches must now move from co-operation to clear commitment to each other, in search of the unity for which Christ prayed, and in common evangelism and service of the world.

The 320 of us who had the privilege of being part of Swanwick 1987 went away somewhat euphoric, but we knew that the real test would lie in translating that euphoria into action. We had to share our vision with those who were still unaware that prayers had been answered and would go on being answered. If we trusted the Spirit to lead us into all truth then the amended words of the 'Not Strangers But Pilgrims' prayer could become a reality in our country, 'For we are strangers no longer, but pilgrims together on the way to your Kingdom.'

5

Instruments for God – or Talking Shops?

Mountain-top experiences can be a problem, and when we left Swanwick, many of us were immediately back into a world which neither knew nor cared that we had taken part in a week capable of changing Christian Britain. But the small Steering Group was luckier. We withdrew further into Derbyshire and its Peak District to review and finalise the conference report. We went to Cliff College, the Methodist Training College at Calver, and for thirty-six hours stayed together savouring some of the highlights of the conference, but very aware of the problems and opportunities now presented to our Churches.

The Next Steps

The immediate task was to get the Swanwick Declaration into as many hands and minds as possible. It was headed 'No longer Strangers – Pilgrims!' and then, after some research, we added (in Welsh), *'Nid Dieithriad Mwyach – Pererinion!'* and finally after a lot more research (in Gaelic) *'Luchd – Turuis – Conhla!'* If this makes the point that this Declaration was for every Christian in the land the linguistic research was worthwhile! It was agreed that every denomination would send copies to their member Churches to be read as a pastoral letter on a Sunday in September or early October, or publicised in other ways. In some cases this worked well, but in others the idea of a pastoral letter to be read in Church was novel, and sadly quite a number of people never heard the Declaration and are ignorant of its contents and importance to this day.

Next we had the much bigger job of preparing the full conference report, first for the Lambeth meeting of Church leaders on September 16th, and then for circulation around the thirty-two denominations themselves for their urgent consideration. Perhaps the most remarkable part of the final document which was published in November 1987, was the flow-chart setting out a possible timetable of events which led up to these two brief statements: 'August 31st, 1990; ring out the Old! September 1st, 1990; ring in the New!'

This was a brave prediction in 1987: the next three years were to be full of consultations and votes and yet that timetable has been kept to and the inauguration of the new national bodies takes place on Saturday September 1st, 1990. Churches Together in England (CTE) at London. Action of Churches Together in Scotland (ACTS) at Dunblane, and Churches Together in Wales (CYTUN) at Aberystwyth. The inauguration of the Council of Churches for Britain and Ireland (CCBI) is on Saturday, September 8th, at Liverpool.

The report then outlines the main findings and feelings of the conference.

We have a deeper appreciation of the visible and historical characteristics of each Church and denomination. There are differences of doctrine and discipline, of spirituality and patterns of worship. We need to acknowledge both the things that unite us, and those that divide us if the Inter-Church Process is to take us on the path to unity in truth and love. As we travel the way of Pilgrims we must continue to study together the important issues that divide us (e.g. the nature of the Church, authority, ministry) and celebrate the gift of that unity which has already been received. (*Churches Together in Pilgrimage* page 11)

The Swanwick report stresses that the urgency and priority of the task is mission and service:

Our task as the Body of Christ is to go out in love with the whole Gospel for the whole world. We are challenged both to share the Good News by our words and also to be the Good News by our life and actions, as we respond to the call of holiness.

In the future this work needs to be common policy at all levels and in all places:

There are ways of co-operation without amalgamation. We are called to trust one another and to take 'holy risks' for the sake of common mission. Competitive evangelism is no longer acceptable, and on every agenda the first question should be 'is this a priority?' and the second 'how can we do this together?' (*Ibid*, page 13).

Everything else in the report is there to help and sustain appropriate ecumenical growth and common action in village, town, city and county. It is worthy of note that though the Steering Group tidied up the report in a few places and drew out a few further implications, it remains substantially as it was written on the last evening of the conference by four lay men and women. This is not a high-powered document processed by ecclesiastical civil servants or theologians: it is the words of grass-roots Christians who had to go back and live them out in their own local situation.

Churches Together in Pilgrimage

The Swanwick report, when published in April 1988, received widespread support and encouraged the Steering Group to proceed to a definitive set of proposals to be put to all the denominations. This was worked on throughout 1988 and the final proposals, *The Next Steps for Churches Together in Pilgrimage*, was published early in 1989. This went to all the thirty-two Churches asking for their final decision before the end of the year.

The proposed structures are radical and fully in the spirit of the Swanwick Declaration, and it is a matter of some surprise that almost all Churches who started out together in 1985 have committed themselves to membership of the appropriate bodies. Scottish Baptists have not felt able to take part, and the position of the Welsh Baptists is still unsure at the point of writing. The Irish scene is more complicated, but it is encouraging that the Church of Ireland and the Methodist Church have taken up full membership, and the Roman Catholic Church has asked for observer status and so will be involved. The Presbyterian Church of Ireland is unable to associate itself with the Process but remains as a partner in the Ballymascanlon talks.

Some who have been working within their own denominations promoting the new scheme have been pleased at the way its recommendations have been accepted, but others fear that their true import and real implications have not yet come home to everyone. To quote one experienced Church official, 'We have said yes, but I wonder if we realised what we have done; Swanwick still has not got into the bloodstream of many of our people. We have got so used to being polite in ecumenical matters that some may not have taken it seriously enough.' However all the due processes of decision making in each body have been carried out, and in most cases the vote in favour has been massive, and this should bode well for their implementation in the coming months and years.

In this chapter I set out briefly the main points of the proposals which come into effect on September 1st, 1990. At the end of August 1990 the present British Council of Churches, the Scottish Churches' Council and the Council of Churches for Wales, cease functioning as such after serving the Kingdom of God well for nearly fifty years. This will not be easy, as some people have become very attached to the present structures, and may have given a lifetime of professional or voluntary service to them. But the message is now clear: 'Ring out the Old, and Ring in the New.'

The Spirit of the Proposals

The principles which underlie these new 'ecumenical

instruments' whether at national, county, town or village level are the same and the most fundamental is this:

> This new scheme requires a shift in the thinking, feeling and action of our Churches from ecumenism as an extra, which absorbs energy, to ecumenism as a dimension of all that we do, which releases energy through the sharing of resources (*Churches Together in Pilgrimage, op. cit.*, page 3).

The rest of the report then unpacks that seemingly simple statement. 'Ecumenism as an extra' describes well where many people are today; we run our own Churches and organisations and, if we have got any energy or time left over, we go along to the Council of Churches, and either support it and its events, or feel guilty if we don't. The Councils of Churches are seen as an 'extra' alongside the real work of the Church, and some have become fed up with their cumbersome and time consuming machinery and structures.

In fact though Councils of Churches have achieved a great deal, some not functioning well, and a few are standing in the way of real united Church action. 'Too often in the past the councils of Churches have served as an "alibi" for the Churches, allowing a relatively small number of people to pursue pieces of work in the name of the Churches, yet which the Churches have been entirely free to overlook or repudiate as they wish' (*Churches Together in Pilgrimage, op. cit.*, page 89).

The new proposals seek to create fairly simple 'instruments' to enable Churches to carry them out together, and not leave it to a few keen individuals who are like-minded, even if drawn from different denominations. So often it has been an 'us' and 'them' situation, with 'them' being the ecumenical Council over and against 'us' the individual Church. In future the ecumenical body will bring representatives of the Churches together to consult and establish priorities, but it will be the Churches themselves that make the decisions, and then authorise and empower an ecumenical body, or one of the Churches or their agencies, to act on behalf of everyone. Not everything ecumenical must be done by an ecumenical body as long as the Churches themselves are agreed and committed to its being carried out. But in the end the responsibility and authority rest and remain with the Churches themselves. That is why we must have the 'Churches Together', and not just the enthusiasts.

It is not easy to get this across and that is why a new name and image is needed. The term 'Council', though having an honourable history, needs to change as it has come to signify the 'extra' approach to ecumenism. So the new concept and title of 'Churches Together' is growing in acceptance. As yet it is novel and little known but this is changing and titles like 'Churches Together in England' and in other local places are becoming more common and accepted. One of the most recently created 'county instruments' is called 'Churches Together in Devon' and the involvement of the Churches in the Gateshead National Garden Festival is using the title of 'Churches Together' for their joint witness at this big event. The name of the new Welsh body 'CYTUN' can best be translated as 'together', and the new Scottish body 'ACTS' has certainly a lot to live up to. Words alone will not now suffice!

What's in a name? The answer is a good deal, provided that it symbolises a new and different approach. The Churches have now committed themselves at the national level and the question is how best to spread this new title and concept, while still honouring and respecting the older title and approach. It is important to see these changes as new marching orders for people on the move, and not just ecclesiastical joinery or more layers of bureaucracy. The challenge of mission must be the driving force, rather than that of keeping the show on the road. Unless this spirit comes through, at all levels, the new instruments will be as useless as a spade rusting in the garden shed, or a violin which is never taken out of its case to be played. They will not do the job they are designed for unless they are used by Christians to help build the Kingdom of God in each and every place, using all the many and varied resources of God's Church.

The Local Level

If they are to work, the Proposals must be seen to express the will of the Churches as a whole, and the decisions of Church leaders must be rooted in widespread participation of lay people. Section six of *Churches Together in Pilgrimage* ('Participation and Representation', page 19) is given over to this point, and the planning of the Lent 1990 study course with its theme 'Turning Points' seeks again to harness this lay and local initiative and response.

Each of the four national sections of the proposals begins at the same place – namely the local. The lesson seems to be learnt and the paramount importance of the local comes across clearly. This means infinite variety as each locality has different backgrounds, opportunities and unique problems, but in every case there is a next step to be taken 'hand in hand' whatever their local starting point may be. It is expected that the six hundred existing English LEPs will continue to increase, and that the smaller number in Wales and Scotland will also grow. The form of local ecumenism that is growing most rapidly is that of the Local Covenant, whereby existing Churches, usually still based in their own buildings, covenant together with others in their locality in common mission to, and service of, their local community.

The Proposals recognise that the biggest area of adjustment will lie with the thousand or more local Councils of Churches in Britain as a whole. They have achieved so much in the past fifty years, but they are bound to be affected both from 'below', and 'above': 'below' because many of them are too big to become effective local units of ecumenical mission; and 'above' because in England they will now relate to their intermediary or county bodies, rather than as before directly to the bodies replacing the British Council of Churches. In Scotland and Wales, however, being more compact countries, they will be linked directly to their new national body.

Many of our large city Councils will continue to have a vital role with or alongside the county body in relating the Churches to the whole life and activity of the city. Cities like Bristol, Birmingham and Sheffield have a long history of Councils of Churches, often with full or part-time staff, which have served their cities well and also performed a co-ordinating role with smaller Councils within the city.

But middle-sized Councils of Churches are finding their new role lies mainly in supporting or setting up groups of local Churches within their area to work together at that level. They themselves may then play a smaller role than in the past, especially in such things as organising services and meetings. They will continue to have a vital co-ordinating role, especially in work such as with Christian Aid, industrial and social mission and agencies, and in encouraging 'Churches Together' at every level of their town life.

The County Level

The newest 'level' of ecumenism in England is the county or intermediary body. This now exists in some shape or form in every county and most metropolitan areas. One of the most constructive gatherings held to prepare for the final Swanwick conference was called by CCLEPE at the All Saints Pastoral Centre at London Colney just before Christmas 1986. Denominational leaders, theologians and Ecumenical Officers were brought together to examine 'ecumenical oversight'. In more ordinary terms, to work out how the denominations can best exercise leadership and care for the local areas that are already united or uniting. It was a unanimous recommendation from this gathering that a single national body was too remote to do this work effectively, and that in England at any rate, the major input of new resources should be at county level. At this level there needs to be an effective instrument which brings together the local Church leaders (bishops, chairmen and moderators) and representative clergy and laity for regular and informal meetings, and that they employ an Ecumenical

Officer whose first loyalty and responsibility is to the combined Church leaders and to this body, and whose executive arm he or she should be.

The Swanwick Report later accepted this recommendation, which was already functioning well in large cities like Liverpool and Birmingham, and also in some largely rural areas like Lincolnshire and Cumbria. While the Ecumenical Officer is dependent on the support and encouragement of his or her leaders, none-the-less the impact of such a person is considerable. The so-called 'Merseyside Miracle' is dependent on the close co-operation shown by Archbishop Derek Worlock, Bishop David Shepherd and Free Church Moderator, presently the Rev Dr John Newton. But they would be the first to acknowledge that part of the reason for this transformation is that sixteen years ago the bold decision was taken to appoint a full-time ecumenically financed Ecumenical Officer. A succession of such officers, drawn from the ranks of the individual Churches, have had the training and the enthusiasm, to translate vision into practice, and there is a distinct correlation between the areas with effective Ecumenical Officers, and the areas of growth of local ecumenism.

So a key proposal in the English section of the report (*Churches Together in Pilgrimage, op. cit.*, page 32) is that the forty-nine county or metropolitan areas be given the resources of money and people to be the effective agents of 'Churches Together' at their levels. Such bodies do now exist but some are still very young and inexperienced, and some still have little power or trust. Some local Councils of Churches hardly know they exist, or what they are for. This is changing as all the local Church groupings within their areas start to relate directly through the county bodies rather than to the British Council itself.

Perhaps Milton Keynes has gone furthest along this road, and though it is only part of a county, it has a structure that many areas can study with profit and then adapt. After a recent visit to this new Buckinghamshire city, the Archbishop of Canterbury was reported as saying, 'I have seen the future, and it works.'

The future for Milton Keynes is that in 1991 they hope to replace their full-time Ecumenical Officer with a full-time Ecumenical Moderator, who will be the focus of unity in the city and its area, and whose exercising of 'Ecumenical Episcope' will be accepted alongside that of the denominational leaders. This commitment is also being shown in the building of the city centre Church of Christ the Cornerstone, a 'Cathedral' for all the Churches of the city at a cost of over four million pounds. Not all areas are ready for these developments, but even Milton Keynes wasn't built in a day! It has become an ecumenical city, because it contains the largest concentration of LEPs in the country. First came the decision of all the denominational leaders to work together in the new city; then the real breakthrough came with the appointment of a full-time Ecumenical Officer. When he was in post the number of LEPs multiplied and then came the structure to support them. In turn this has encouraged even more local ecumenical growth. This is increasingly the pattern of many local areas in all parts of the country.

Churches Together in England, Scotland and Wales

Scotland and Wales already have national bodies in existence but on September 1st, 1990 these will change to Action of Churches Together in Scotland (*Churches Together in Pilgrimage, op. cit.*, pages 49–59) and Churches Together in Wales (CYTUN) (*ibid.*, pages 61–76). A completely new body for England will also commence on that date, Churches Together in England (*ibid.*, pages 27–47). Each of these will have the same basic approach and structure, but will vary according to the size of the country and the balance of the denominations and other local factors.

The new instruments will seek to balance the necessity of having a small body that can act fairly quickly in certain agreed matters on behalf of 'Churches Together', with a larger body in which the lay and the local voice can be heard. The lessons and experiences of the past three years have made their contribution, and in each country there will be a large residential gathering, a Scottish Forum, an English Assembly and a Welsh *Y Gymanfa*, about every other year, and their role will be important. These large gatherings are intended to be the eyes and ears of the Churches, so that people involved in both local ecumenism and those engaged in special apostolic work in the Churches (e.g. social responsibility, education, justice and peace, and development work) can share their experiences and celebrate their pilgrimage in faith.

Decisions are taken by the Churches according to their normal pattern of authority. The Enabling Group (known by different titles in the three national bodies) assists the Churches in reaching those decisions which are proper to them and then enables the Churches to undertake together those tasks which will lead them into deeper and more visible unity. In other words, those tasks which will promote the mission of Christ's Church.

Each national body will have its own small headquarters in London, Swansea and Dunblane, and they will work closely with, and hopefully co-ordinate and encourage, local ecumenism and mission in their own nation.

Ireland

No new instruments are proposed within Ireland itself (*Churches Together in Pilgrimage, op. cit.*, pages 77–78) but the main ecumenical structures will continue as before, and it is hoped that gradually some of the experiences set out in the new instruments will take shape in Ireland as well. However, most of the Churches there will relate to the new British and Irish Council either as full members, or with 'observer' status, and there is a determination on both sides of the Irish Sea that this body will encourage growing interchange of experiences and persons. The Irish have held the Ballymascanlon talks for many years, and these have included Roman Catholics and Protestants as full members. The English, Scots and Welsh will hope to learn' from this Irish experience.

Most of the working out of the Swanwick declaration will therefore be carried out at these levels in the four nations where local concerns are paramount; to the man and woman in the pew these are the ones that will most directly interest and concern them. But important as the work of the local Church is, there are other areas of life and of the Churches' mission that can best be debated, decided and acted upon at the highest level that can be set up.

The Council of Churches for Britain and Ireland

Because at first sight this looks rather like the British Council of Churches it can be asked 'is there anything new in CCBI?' In fact the proposals are new (*Churches Together in Pilgrimage, op. cit.*, pages 79–104) but they also contain much that is old and has proved valuable. It should be noted that it is still a 'Council of Churches' and not 'Churches Together', and this is important. The new body is the meeting place for all the many diverse Churches in the four nations, and unlike the national bodies will be made up almost entirely of people appointed by the thirty-two denominations themselves, though it is hoped that at least half of them will also represent their Churches on their appropriate national ecumenical body.

The Council's role will be mainly in co-ordinating whatever must properly be addressed at a British and Irish level. One of the great concerns of the Swanwick conference was that of 'developing complementary agendas, so that both levels of instruments would be part of an integrated operation with an agreed division of labour' (*ibid.*, page 88). This will not be easy and may need adjustment in the future. 'The four national ecumenical bodies will have a primary care for evangelism and joint outreach in the four nations and a general concern for the way in which their members understand the nature of the Church' (*ibid.*, page 97). CCBI will come into operation when the Churches in all four nations need to work together, especially on matters of public concern in British and Irish issues.

The main occasion for giving direction and general

approval will be a meeting every two years of a Swanwick-type conference to be called the 'Assembly', and it is envisaged that there will be about 350 members drawn from every Church according to size; i.e. Church of England forty-five, Church of Scotland thirty, Presbyterian Church of Wales six, and so on. There would also be a definite policy to make sure that the smaller Churches do not feel left out or overpowered by the big denominations.

The working out of policy priority agreed by the Assembly would rest with the 'Church Representatives Meeting'. This smaller body of about sixty members would meet three times a year and would bring together the senior members appointed to represent their Churches for this purpose. The relationship and balance between the 'Church leader' and the 'lay voice' is going to be crucial at all levels in the new instruments. Where immediate action has to be taken, the Church Representatives Meeting must be trusted to act; but it is hoped that this will be balanced by their being part of the Assembly when it meets to discern new directions. The balance of executive action, and democratic consultation will not satisfy everyone, especially the denominations that are wary of 'Church leaders' and in some cases claim not to have any!

To try and meet this point the third part of the carefully balanced structure being set up is the day to day 'Steering Committee', and this will have six members elected by the Assembly and six by the Church Representatives Meeting with the senior executive officers of the four National Bodies and the General Secretary of the Council.

As with the British Council of Churches, many other bodies will relate to CCBI, and draw support from it. Working with the Council will be a series of networks, commissions and agencies. Each of these will be important, and at times drawing from and impinging on the Churches at all levels of their life.

Christian Aid and CAFOD will play important roles as 'Agencies in Association with the Council' as will the Committee for Relations with People of Other Faiths, the Community and Race Relations Unit, and Opportunities for

Volunteering. Many of them actually function within the building at Lower Marsh near Waterloo Station in south London where the British Council of Churches has had its head office since 1987 and where both CCBI and CTE will have their headquarters.

Instruments for God?

The Inter-Church meeting and its Steering Group have been responsible for implementing the decisions of the Swanwick conference and also assessing the reactions of all the different Churches to the proposals over the past three years. Throughout, their meetings have been characterised by a spirit of prayer and readiness to seek God's will as the representatives have listened to one another expressing very different positions. These new instruments have been forged in an atmosphere of growing trust and willingness to state one's own convictions, but also to pay real regard to other points of view.

But already some people are asking what all this long list of structures and meetings has got to do with the Kingdom of God. It would be easy to be highly impatient and critical and see it as an excuse for a lot of people going to a lot of meetings, rather than getting on with the task of building the Kingdom of God in our land. Time may prove that this is so, and that the Churches have failed to create a new way of sharing in common mission and ended up again with a way of Churches talking to each other and nothing more.

But they are intended to be instruments for the furtherance of God's Kingdom and must be judged on that basis and on no other. Though many hope they are truly inspired by God's Holy Spirit, and we now have over fifty years of hard experience in this work, they are still structures created by fallible human beings. Their success or failure will be judged not so much by the structures which I have tried briefly to set out in this chapter, but by the practical working-out that I shall try to describe in the next two. The proof of this particular pudding will be very much in the local eating!

6

Relationships on the 'C Scale'

Earlier chapters have briefly sketched the ecumenical events of the eighties. In this and the following chapters the focus is on the future and how the events and changes of the eighties can affect Christian work and mission at all levels of life but especially at the most important, the local.

For some years ecumenists have used the 'C Scale' to assess the warmth of relationships between the Churches. The scale starts at the bottom and then ascends:

Competition
Co-existence
Co-operation
Commitment
Communion

The Swanwick Declaration requires *'that, as a matter of policy at all levels and in all places, our Churches must now move from co-operation to clear commitment to each other, in search of the unity for which Christ prayed, and in common evangelism and service of the world'*. We are all asked to move up the scale, but to bear in mind that the top line is communion.

In some places there is no need to 'move up' as those working in them are already 'committed'. Committed, that is, within their own immediate circle, but they need to recognise that this circle may exclude others and should now be re-drawn so as to include them. However, following the

call from Swanwick, others have said, with varying degrees
of cynicism, 'We can't move up from something we have
not yet arrived at.' Sadly this is true, and there are some
places lower down the 'C Scale' where competition is not
yet extinct.

Throughout Britain and Ireland the local picture is tremen-
dously varied, and part of the penalty of not having any
overall reunion scheme is that it will continue to be so. There
are variations between the four nations themselves, and if
England gives the appearance of being a bit further up the
scale than the other three nations, there are some glorious
local exceptions in Scotland, Wales and Ireland. It is also true
that there are whole areas in all four countries where co-
existence is still the only true term to use. As was said in
the previous chapter, there are hopeful signs of change where
the Church leaders have themselves moved up the 'C Scale',
and then empowered an Ecumenical Officer to instigate and
encourage the local Churches to follow their example.

The influence of the existing Councils of Churches, and
the Local Ecumenical Projects on their own neighbouring
areas has also been important, but it is depressing to find
that Churches almost next door to one another live in total
ignorance of what each other does. In some cases this
ignorance is the result of a deliberate rejection of working
with any other Church, or of wanting to know what they
do – including those of one's own denomination! Some
clergy and ministers in all Churches have a fear of shared
or collaborative ministry and are only happy if they 'run
their own show'. This may be rationalised by all sorts of
theological reasoning, but at heart it is psychological rather
than theological. Many lay people find this very frustrating,
and while their own attachment to bricks and mortar may
also hinder ecumenism, they do not necessarily have the
same fear of working with others.

These traits run through every denomination and are
human rather than ecclesiastical. However, there are some
denominational factors and characteristics which are
sufficiently general to be worth spelling out, however
briefly.

The Church of England

The Church of England has a far greater number of clergy and buildings than anyone else, and in the countryside is often the only apparently functioning Church for many miles. As with other Churches its resources are more and more stretched, and it is not unknown for a country priest to have up to eight or nine small parishes to look after with all the administrative and custodial responsibilities that go with multiple care. But the Church of England still holds to its parochial system and even if the leadership of the Church wanted to give it up, many parishioners would resist tooth and nail. The Church of England and many of the people of England see it as the Church you belong to if you are not anything else. When asked on admission into hospital 'What religion are you?' the standard reply of about seventy per cent of people is 'C of E'!

This gives it a missionary base far wider than that of any other Church in England, and although more Churches are becoming eclectic in their membership, the day to day care of parishioners is, for most of them, their task and opportunity. The Church of England tries to relate to, and represent its own local community, and this is the characteristic contribution that it can bring to local ecumenical mission.

But it is also the Church that has been mainly responsible for the rejection of many reunion schemes, and it can still have a decisive influence on local ecumenism for good or ill. The greatest danger locally and nationally is when it decides to do something on its own, and only afterwards invites others to take part! If the parish Church will not take part in ecumenical activities, then constructive local unity is almost impossible to achieve, however much the other Churches may want to work together. A lot of responsibility now rests on Church of England clergy to make the new ecumenical structures work, and it will need a good deal of episcopal and other encouragement, if not actual pressure, for the instruments to become accepted, trusted and used.

One hopeful factor in the present situation is that the Church of England has just accepted a new ecumenical framework in the passing of the Ecumenical Canons B43 and B44. After the dissensions of the past it is good to record that these were accepted overwhelmingly by every diocese and by the General Synod itself. The first Canon (B43) allows a great deal of sharing of buildings and life in any parish that wishes it, and the second (B44) goes further in making legal the hundreds of Local Ecumenical Projects and much that has been happening in them over the past twenty years. There is little that is new in either Canon, but it is the first time that the Church of England has recognised in its laws that it is now in partnership with other Churches in mission to this country. Some see the Canons as excessively legalistic and still too restrictive, but it does mean that many practices which were formerly seen as experimental can now be carried out with the full approval of the Church.

The way is open for even the most law abiding parish of the Church of England to move from co-operation to commitment. There are still some who do not appreciate the opportunities legally open to them, but the Canons could not have come at a more opportune moment. The new structures encourage a move forward, and the new Canons allow this to a greater extent than many people yet realise. As we have seen in earlier chapters, there has been a good deal of impatience with the Church of England authorities and some of this will continue, but there has also been a real danger of ecumenism creating new splits and divisions rather than healing old ones. The Canons now encourage more people to share with their fellow Christians, and to do it under legal authority.

One of the sorrows of the Church of England, at least until recently, has been that the section of the Church at present showing the greatest liveliness and growth, namely the Evangelicals, has not always been so actively involved in ecumenism as others. One of the priorities of the Decade of Evangelism must be to help Evangelicals to see how much other Churches need their insights and gifts working in and through these new structures. Canons can allow, but only the Spirit can inspire.

Another sadness is the internal bitterness being created over the ordination of women to the priesthood. I do not think that many now doubt this will eventually come about here as in many other parts of the Anglican Communion. But its coming is certainly causing great tension and deflecting the Church from its main task of evangelism. The ecumenical argument is being used by people on both sides of the debate, some pointing to the need for unity with the Roman Catholic and Orthodox Churches who still hold to the tradition of centuries of a solely male priesthood; others pointing to the need to preach the Gospel to a world newly aware of the unity of male and female in Christ, and to share with many Protestant Churches in the development of an equality in ministry between male and female. However, it is surely up to the Anglican Communion to make its own decision, and to remember that our partners in the Gospel are many and varied. This is part of the diversity we have to live with, and perhaps the ecumenical movement with its new-found emphasis on diversity within unity, can point a way forward rather than holding us back.

The Roman Catholic Church

The active arrival of the Roman Catholic Church on the ecumenical scene has brought the biggest change of all. Until some years ago the ecumenical movement at all levels largely excluded Roman Catholics. This was partly from their unreadiness to participate in projects and schemes which seemed to them to be based on principles different from their own and in which there seemed there was sometimes a less than warm welcome. There were some notable exceptions, but being a Church with an international structure of authority there was not the same freedom to experiment, and there was some mistrust on all sides, bred by past history. Local ecumenical partnerships were set up without people even thinking of consulting the local Roman Catholic Church. 'Oh they would not be able to take part, even if they wanted to' reflected the co-existence level in most places. But still it must be recorded that a shared Anglican-Roman Catholic Church was built at Cippenham in Slough over twenty-three years ago, and others have followed – though this is not always the great advance that some hoped for.

The Second Vatican Council opened the door for great change. But it needed the Pope's visit in 1982 and the leadership of bishops like Alan Clark and archbishops like Derek Worlock, the patient work of Dick Stewart and Dennis Corbishley (until their premature deaths), the theological progress in the ARCIC talks, and the widespread lay involvement in Lent '86 for the Roman Catholic Church in England and Wales to take its ecumenical initiative in 1984, to become a full partner in 'Not Strangers But Pilgrims' in 1985, and then for Cardinal Hume to make such an impact at Swanwick in 1987.

Not that the scene has changed overnight; there are still places in all four countries where the Swanwick Declaration is either unknown or viewed with great alarm. Habits do not change quickly, and it is up to non-Catholics to realise just how big a change their Catholic friends are being asked to make. I was talking recently to a local priest who was telling off his people for not attending a joint service in a Parish Church, and gently reminding him that it was not all that long ago that his Church was teaching them that it could have been a matter of confession if his people had taken part!

We must remember this historical perspective and not be surprised when sometimes progress seems painfully slow. There are understandable concerns about whether ecumenical dialogue could lead to a 'watering down' of their teaching in favour of a 'lowest common denomination' Christianity. This is especially true of their principles on morality and understanding of the sacraments.

As in the Church of England, some diocesan bishops are more encouraging than others. For instance the joint Roman Catholic, Anglican, and Methodist confirmation service held in the LEP in Thamesmead in the Southwark Archdiocese, would not yet be permitted in some other diocese and is a topic of much discussion. This parallels the uneven way ecumenism has developed in the Church of England. In Cardinal Hume's words 'it is not often realised how much diversity there is inside the Catholic Church'.

The Roman Catholics, more than any other Church, are insisting upon a new approach to ecumenical working; they are rightly worried about any structure that sets itself over against the Churches themselves. This was one of the reasons why they would not join the outgoing British Council of Churches. They have brought a strong theological and ecclesiological influence to bear on the shaping of all aspects of the new instruments, and will therefore have a vested interest in making them work.

The Roman Catholic bishops, or their representatives, are now involved in all but one (South Yorkshire, where it is confidently expected that they will be founding members of the South Yorkshire Ecumenical Council) of the new county bodies, and at the moment four of the full-time county Ecumenical Officers are Catholic priests or lay people.

It is a matter of regret that some local priests are not able to give more time and help to ecumenical affairs, but this is in part because of a big problem which affects most of our denominations – namely ecumenical geography. It is also because they are very fully stretched and are afraid that ecumenism will absorb energy rather than release it!

But in more and more places Roman Catholic clergy and laity are bringing a freshness and enthusiasm lacking in some other Churches. Some of us who have been living with these issues most of our lives may think this at times a bit naïve – but how refreshing it is, and how much needed if we are really to get a new spirit moving.

Other Churches in England

The majority of the Free Churches (together with most members of the Baptist Union who were the first to vote on the proposals early in 1989) are deeply committed to the

Inter-Church Process. The United Reformed Church especially has made sacrifices for this over the past few years. Some in these Churches feel that the failure of unity talks should have led first to a closer unity within the Free Churches, rather than the wider working together now proposed. But while this was not seen as the best way forward at national level, there are a number of united Churches at the local level with effective sharing of buildings and ministers. There are also a number of united Methodist and URC 'Areas' – most of Wiltshire is covered by these proving that different Church administrations can be harmonised.

Locally, the Free Church Federal Councils are working out how best to continue in relationships with other groupings, and while some of the smaller Churches welcome a Free Church umbrella body, others do not see the necessity for such a body as distinct from a more all-embracing ecumenical instrument, despite the continuing need for arrangements to be made about Free Church Hospital Chaplaincies.

There are a few places where the local 'House or Community Church' has shown a willingness to be involved, and no local 'Churches Together' should be formed without them being invited to take part in the preparatory discussions. While some will reject the offer, others will be glad to meet and begin to build bridges of confidence, and a few will be willing to enter into a Local Covenant. As more of them acquire buildings of their own and find the need of some recognised pattern for ministers and training, they are realising that they have more in common with other Churches than they at first thought. If the Churches in a Local Covenant are able to accept that the Spirit is given in different ways to different people, and it is not just 'an ecumenism of the like minded', their partnership can be very profitable especially in the field of mission and outreach.

Churches in Scotland and Wales

In Scotland the Inter-Church Process has seen the start of real co-operation between the Church of Scotland and the Roman Catholic Church, and the Church of Scotland has opportunities similar to the Church of England, and may have an even more central role in the life of their nation than any other comparable Church in Britain. However, though there is a greater cohesion among the Churches than in England, in some of the smaller Scottish Churches there is also a greater fear of 'Rome'. Much is happening at all levels and there have been many 'ecumenical firsts' since the Swanwick Declaration.

Wales continues to have the great advantage of its unique Covenant at national level between a number of Churches. The Church in Wales is fully involved in this, and it enables the Churches concerned to do more together than is possible elsewhere. It does not cover all the Churches in Wales, but in all there are now sixty Local Ecumenical Projects and CYTUN intends to give priority to enabling further developments and has set up a working party to plan and co-ordinate this work.

The local scene throughout Britain is very varied, but these brief comments on a few of the main denominational differences may help in understanding some of their local manifestations. I want now to tackle the issue of 'ecumenical geography', then to look at four very different areas of ecumenical work in our country, and finally to set out simple guidelines that may help some local Churches harmonise their work and mission.

Ecumenical Geography

At every level this is a problem; no one Church's boundaries ever seem to coincide with anyone else's and this is a direct result of centuries of division. Some areas and boundaries (such as the URCs) have been set up recently, while others date from medieval times. When we were planning the possible county bodies we found that the only place where boundaries made any sense was in Cornwall, and even there it is only the Anglican diocese and the Methodist district which are the same! Baptist General Superintendents cover vast areas and the United Reformed Church's Moderators have a big problem as there are only fourteen of them to cover England, Scotland and Wales; and in the West Midlands the Moderator has to relate to no less than seven county bodies. An ability to drive like Jehu must be an essential qualification for the job.

During the Inter-Church Process considerable thought was given to whether or not we should all embark on a great campaign to get our boundaries conterminous. It would be wonderful if it could happen, but when one considers the difficulties the Church of England has about changing a single parish boundary, or the amount of time the Methodist Church spent discussing and then rejecting a central London district, one has to sympathise with the view that we have not the time or the energy to spare at the present and therefore we must adapt as best we can. There are some practical ways in which we can improve our ecumenical geography, but in the main we are stuck with most of our peculiar boundaries for this century at least.

While this is true at county level, it is also true at the more local level. In the town of Dronfield in Derbyshire where I am now, we recognise that we are most fortunate because we are an established community which has grown to 27,000 people, but all our Churches serve the same geographical area. To serve our town and its surrounding villages we have an Anglican team ministry of five Churches, a Roman Catholic parish, as well as full-time ministers of Baptist, Methodist, United Reformed Churches and the Oaks Fellowship. This means that our Churches, and some smaller ones as well, all have one thing in common; our primary mission is to our town and its community. Although some of the outlying villages do feel a bit left out, this bond of common geography and identity is very important and most helpful for the mission of the Church.

An important ingredient in successful local ecumenism

is that of affirming the place and role of each congregation in a local unity which is bigger than the individual Church, but not so vast as to be meaningless. The creation of the right sized geographical unit is perhaps the most important single factor for fruitful ecumenical partnership. Many existing Ecumenical Council areas are, at the moment, too big to be effective instruments of Church life. In future their main role will probably be in helping to find, define, and then encourage geographical 'sub units' where local ecumenism can flourish in relation to their own community.

Rural Ecumenism

In rural areas in England, the Church of England is often the only Church with anything like a full complement of ordained ministers and buildings. Although commuters (and computers!) have changed village life, many places are still real communities however small, and the Church must seek to relate to them and serve them. There may be only a single Church in many small villages and one should think in terms of families working together rather than Churches working as one. In the booklet *Christian Unity in the Village* (a BCC publication in 1987) there are stories of very effective working together at the village level. Let me give a couple of other examples which are far from being unique.

In a village in Kent the local Methodist chapel had dry rot (a very effective spur sometimes to ecumenical advance) and so had to be closed; the eight members remained as a Methodist class meeting, but became part of the parish church congregation. The Church paid their Methodist dues, and the nearest Methodist minister came twice a year to preach and celebrate and was available to take part in Methodist weddings or funerals. Under new regulations two of the Methodists were able to be full members of the Parochial Church Council, and more recently they have become eligible to be members of the Deanery Synod. But this pattern will only work where it is accepted that people's most effective place of Christian witness is in their own local community, not regularly driving eight miles to their nearest denominational church.

Administratively it may seem that the best way forward is to choose one village church and then 'bus' people in so as to bring individuals from a number of villages together, but in practice this seldom works because of the failure to recognise the great importance of local identity. Church and chapel may not always have got on well together in every village, but they often have more in common with each other than with members of their own denomination who live in the next village; after all who knows – they may have been on different sides in the Civil War! Ecumenical ways of relating rural Christians to their community are even more important than in town.

In some villages there is still more than one place of worship, and as long as the buildings are water-tight and not too expensive to maintain it is good to have both in use. But the combined congregations could fit into either of the buildings. So a pattern has emerged of a 'winter church' and a 'summer church'. The beautiful old and rather draughty parish church serves the combined congregations from Easter to Harvest, and then the smaller but warmer chapel takes over (except usually for Christmas Day itself and the occasional winter wedding!). Much of the opposition from smaller Churches to combining lies in a fear of losing a very precious building and the identity that goes with it, and if some way can be found that affirms its continuing role in the local community, a way forward in unity can be achieved. But beware, events in the countryside need to mature rather slowly!

The growth of ecumenical house groups has been another way in which working together is being achieved in some villages, and in these as in local prayer groups, more and more Roman Catholics are playing leading roles. Money raising is also a way of bringing people together and nearly all events 'for the church' will call forth support from all local Christians as well as those who are 'non-attenders'.

Whilst ecumenism in the towns and cities may need

formal covenants and instruments, in the villages a more informal way of working is usually required. The foundation must be the same; trust between all those taking part, and a shared concern bigger than just continuing our own Church life and paying its quota. United mission is needed in every community regardless of size.

Urban Ecumenism

We have already seen that Churches in a smallish town have a lot going for them because it is an identifiable community with its own local loyalties, a ready-made community within which the Churches may work. Many towns have more than one Anglican church, and the greatest division can be between these, as over the years they have sought to cater for a variety of Anglican practice, both 'high' and 'low'. It may be that the challenge of a wider commitment bringing in a fuller range of worship and practice, may enable even this to be overcome.

In some small towns the Roman Catholics either have no church, or no resident priest, and so their priests and people have to relate to a number of local communities and not only where their buildings are situated. One of the happy consequences of the new Church of England Ecumenical Canons is that it allows Roman Catholic services to be held in the parish church, and there are already hundreds of such mass centre arrangements working well, and most with happy 'spin offs' from this relationship. There is also the presence in a few places of the Roman Catholic religious orders, and considerable pioneering ecumenical work has been done, especially by nuns. In some cases their active involvement predates any other local ecumenical commitment by many years.

The problems of ecumenical geography are at their greatest in the large towns and cities. At the top level you have conurbations like Humberside, Merseyside and Tyneside where politics may dictate one authority, but traditional Church and other affiliations often use their river as a boundary. This is also true of London, but there, at the moment, political divisions are even more diverse than ecclesiastical ones!

Each city has its largely depopulated centre with many fine Churches serving a handful of caretakers and thousands of office workers, and then its inner rings of old communities and suburbia, and finally its outer ring of new estates or satellite towns.

In the major conurbations Councils of Churches have been of great importance and will almost certainly continue to function in close collaboration with the newer county bodies, but their most immediate task is to examine and define the most effective local units of ecumenism within their city. In some ways the ideal ecumenical unit is one where there is a Church of each of the major denominations, but not more than about six Churches in all, which then have some local name or district in common to give them a sense of responsibility to that community. Traditionally the parish church had this role on its own, but increasingly it shares this task with other Churches in 'the parish'. In some cities no such clearly definable areas exist, but they are worth searching for and trying to help create. Responsibilities within the denominations should be adapted to match them wherever this is possible. In Nottingham a change of ministerial responsibility within one of the circuits enabled a Methodist minister to work full-time within one such new community, and this made a big difference to all Churches within that locality.

Another example may help. Twenty years ago Swindon started to grow from the old 'God's Wonderful Railway' town of eighty thousand into a modern 'electronics' city of almost two hundred thousand. Those of us working there had to face the fact that the Swindon Council of Churches had to change if it was to be effective in the new town. The Swindon Commission was set up by all the Churches and asked to take a year to report, and it was encouraged to visit as many other similar communities as possible. The Commission was made up of Church leaders, local people who knew the town well, and the Planning Department of the then Swindon Borough. All had an important part to play in the final report which recommended that though the Council should continue, its main role in the future would be co-ordinating and encouraging local ecumenism in seven geographical sub-areas of the town, and relating them to the local authorities. Five geographical communities and their appropriate Churches were identified within the existing town, and two others were designated even though most of the inhabitants at the time were cows! The cows have since departed and were replaced by tens of thousands of people from all over the country as Swindon became one of the fastest growing towns in Britain.

It is, of course, fairly easy to designate as 'ecumenical areas' places that do not yet exist, but it still needed the full commitment of the denominations to see that all new Churches were built on an ecumenical basis. In the five existing areas of the town it was a great help to have this blueprint for the future. Not all the Churches felt able to work fully together in the areas suggested, and still one of the main Anglican Churches is not part of the central team of Churches. But in all the other areas there are now ecumenical Churches or groupings of Churches working together and one of them has just come of age after twenty-one years of being an ecumenical parish.

As in any place there have been ups and downs, and enthusiasms have waxed and waned, but there is no doubt that as a result of that year's 'spade work', everyone knows who they could work with if they wished to do so. That may not exactly bring in the Kingdom of God, but it does help, and certainly Swindon can speak of itself as an 'ecumenical town' working in both the old and new communities, and through the various ecumenical agencies of the area. But this example also shows the weakness of such a situation; every encouragement can be given, but unless a local Church wishes to take part with others it can remain in splendid isolation from its neighbours and simply relate to its own denomination, or sometimes not even to that.

It would be a big step forward if any town or city Council of Churches that has not yet carried out such a survey could do so, and then aid the setting up of more Local Ecumenical Projects within its own catchment area. Many places have already achieved this within their own local area, but unless there is some co-ordinated plan for the whole city or town some Churches coming later on the scene may be left out and have no natural partner to work with. Some Churches see themselves relating to the whole town and having no particular local identity, but this need not stop them having a primary relationship with other 'town Churches' who have a similar role. They should also be encouraging their members, wherever they live, to play an active community role with those Churches that are working together in local groupings.

The value of finding and identifying Churches in relationship to their natural communities is not only a necessity for good ecumenical working, but also for effective local evangelism. While the big central Evangelism Campaign Event may still have a place in the Decade of Evangelism, more and more it is the ongoing local witness of Christians and their Churches which is most vital and this is so much more effective if undertaken jointly. In the Burnley Lane area of Burnley in Lancashire there is one such natural community grouping of Churches in a Local Covenant. The experience of leading an ecumenical mission there in the Autumn of 1988 has 'converted' the leaders and members of a Roman Catholic Religious Order to this way of ecumenical working. They are now refusing to undertake parish missions unless all the local Churches are committed to the enterprise. The experience of sharing in mission preparation and follow-up made the Local Covenant 'come alive' for local Christians and made a great impact on the Order itself.

The same also applies to effective Christian service within a community. City-wide organisation may be needed to relate to Civic Bodies and Social Services, but on the ground many local carers are required and we return to this in the next chapter.

Sector Ecumenism

The Swanwick Declaration says '*It is our conviction that, as a matter of policy at all levels and in all places, our Churches must now move from co-operation to clear commitment to each other, in search of the unity for which Christ prayed, and in common evangelism and service of the world.*' In this book so far I have written mainly in geographical terms, of villages, towns and cities; but in this section I want to refer to 'all levels and places' that are not geographical by definition.

A great deal of official and unofficial ecumenism has gone on over the years in such places as boarding schools, hospitals, prisons and HM Forces. Because chaplaincy in such places serves a very definite and well-defined community it has considerable advantages, and especially in schools there is a long history of close co-operation and most school chapels have exercised 'open Communion' for many years. In the new Church of England Ecumenical Canons there is a special recognition in Canon B44 (section 7) of the important part that such places can play in ecumenical work. I think it was Stafford Prison that became the first official LEP within the Prison Service, but a number of others have followed since.

There has also been close working together in hospital chaplaincies, but here there is a very mobile 'population'. I have had very happy experiences in ecumenical hospital chaplaincy, but I recognise that there are problems caused by the fact that the National Health Service only recognises 'denominational beds' and that chaplains are paid accordingly. I am sure that this is one of the issues that 'Churches Together' must face fairly soon, but in the meantime there is a great deal that a chaplaincy team of clergy, ministers and laity can perform. This is a vital area of united Christian witness where we can meet people at a time of great personal need.

When I was organising Lent '86 I spent a good deal of time with the chaplains in all three of HM Services and came to appreciate the good but difficult job being done by them with members of the Forces and their families. In some places there was excellent co-operation and a ready response to the Inter-Church Process and a good deal of impatience with those who seemed to be holding back closer union. But in others I found the local Church very much under the thumb of the Commanding Officer, and with very little independent life of its own. In these circumstances, and with the additional factor that chaplains move postings fairly frequently, ecumenism is going to need a good deal of help from senior chaplains and from others in the areas where they are stationed. There is a particular opportunity for chaplains working in other parts of the world to relate to the Churches of those countries and so play a part in the wider ecumenical scene.

One of the sector ministries that has embraced ecumenism from its earliest days has been that of social and industrial mission. Because they are always working on the fringe of Church in a largely missionary situation, they are fully aware of the need for the Churches to work together if there is to be any real impact in their sphere of work. I gather that almost all industrial teams are now ecumenical and are registered as Local Ecumenical Projects with the County Ecumenical Council.

Family Ecumenism

Under this heading I want to refer to the most basic unit of ecumenism – the Christian family! While the great majority of Christian families are united in one denomination, there are a growing number of 'mixed marriages' where Christians (and now members of other faiths as well) are happily married but wish to keep to their own religious practices. In some cases this does not produce any great tensions because the partners can take part in each other's worship whenever they wish, but there has been considerable tension where one partner is a Roman Catholic. This was recognised back in 1968 when the Association of Interchurch Families (AIF) was first set up through just such a mixed 'ecumenical marriage' by Martin and Ruth

Reardon (AIF, The Old Bakery, Danehill, Sussex, RH17 7ET).

This has now grown into a world-wide body, and has helped couples and their children. It has also played a small, but significant part, in helping forward the growing trust and understanding between the Churches. In 1983 Ruth Reardon and Melanie Finch edited an important book called *Shared Communion* (Collins 1983) which tells of the strains of such marriages, especially where committed Christian couples and their children cannot receive communion together.

At the twenty-first annual Conference of the Association of Interchurch Families at Swanwick in 1988 a statement was sent on behalf of the Association to the Steering committee of 'Not Strangers But Pilgrims'. Here are two short quotations which indicate how important these 'smallest of ecumenical projects' are:

> We found it very important to worship together in one another's Churches. We found it especially important to be together at the eucharist, even though this is a painful experience when we do not share communion. When we *can* receive communion together we find this strengthens our unity as a couple and as a family. Increasingly we feel it wrong to be separated at the table of the Lord.

Then further on in this very personal and sometimes rather tough statement there comes this now familiar theme:

> We have learned in our marriage that unity does not mean uniformity. Differences enrich our common life. There are, however, some differences between us which threaten the unity of our marriage. In these cases we have to be prepared to discard what is not essential to us, to be ready to give up certain things which we enjoy as individuals, for the sake of living together . . . Equally the Churches need to be prepared to change certain aspects of their life for the sake of unity, if they are really committed to becoming one Church.

Local Ecumenical Instruments

Finally I want to deal with the most effective form of instrument needed at the local level. It may well be in the village that no instrument is needed other than using the local shop, school or village pub, but in most bigger communities some structure is needed.

There may have to be a clearing away of old structures before new ones can begin. In Dronfield we are about to move forward into a new Local Covenant, but to do so we have to wind up a Council of Churches, three Local Ecumenical Projects and a Local Support Group as well! Ecumenism has taken up the time of a lot of people over many years and we are now seeking a way forward which is more effective both in practical terms, and in saving the time of busy people. Some sort of single structure which shows commitment is needed. This means a new form of instrument combining an important role for the clergy and ministers to work and pray together, with a strong enough number of lay voices from each Church for them to feel fully involved. It is not enough to rely on one or two people reporting back to Churches which are still thinking in terms of 'us' and 'them' in united matters.

In many hundreds of communities throughout Britain the concept of a Local Covenant is seen as the way forward, and while not the only way, it does seem to be the best. The actual Covenant needs to be drawn up locally after considerable thought, prayer and discussion about who should sign and what they should sign. There are plenty of models available in such books as the CCLEPE 1986 publication, *Local Church Unity*, and their new publication, *Constitutional Guidelines for a Local Ecumenical Project* (January 1990). This takes into account not only the new Ecumenical Canons of the Church of England, but also those of the Roman Catholics and the Methodist Standing Orders.

In Dronfield we have used as our basis the model provided by Loughton in Essex. We have drawn up our own Covenant, but taken from the Loughton model the idea of two sections within the one overall Covenant, and also used some of the phrases from the Swanwick Declaration itself. We hope that most, if not all, of our local Churches will sign the Covenant itself, and soon after the Covenant is in force, many will then feel able to sign the Further Agreements, so that these Churches will be able to enter into a fuller sharing of ministry and sacraments. It is recognised that as yet it is not possible for the Roman Catholics or indeed the House Church to sign these Further Agreements, but this should neither exclude them from the main Covenant nor hold back the others who are able to enter into fuller sharing. We hope that in future years all may be able to sign the Further Agreements. What we want to avoid at all costs is having two organisations representing different levels of commitment. Our aim is to simplify structures, not create more!

A Covenant must be carefully worked through over a period of time seeking advice from the local county body and from other similar areas, and its actual adoption should be an event which involves many people within the area, and the Church leaders through the County Ecumenical Council. The denominations themselves must recognise that a local Covenant is going to make demands on them, and especially in the future when new ministerial appointments are made to the ecumenical team. This new way of commitment in a Covenant is not just the local Churches being polite to each other; it is the forging of a new pattern of Church life, and it would be a great mistake to rush into it until this is fully understood, and the changes that will have to be made are appreciated both within the Churches and by their supporting denominations. Commitment means just that, and it is better to make haste slowly, than rush into a show piece Covenant which is no more than a piece of paper to be waved or framed!

The drawing up of a Local Covenant will need very careful preparation and a willingness for there to be a 'healing of ecumenical memories' at this level which can be even more important than at the national. In most communities there are deep personal hurts, real or imagined, which people have suffered at the hands or mouths of Christians from other denominations over the years. These 'wounds' can be very deep, and may need much love and care before they can be confessed and gradually healed. Deep and sustained prayer throughout the whole time when a Covenant is being planned is essential. The seeking of God's guidance at every stage in the process and the upholding in prayer of all who are seeking to forward his Kingdom by these new commitments must be paramount both for individuals and Churches. Out of such prayer can come forgiveness and hope, and the new life and trust that are needed if we are to be 'strangers no longer'.

How best 'Churches Together' will function in any local community must depend upon the nature and size of the area, but it should not be too big: in ecumenism, as in so much else 'small is beautiful'. The lessons spelt out in the previous chapter on ecumenical instruments need to be studied, and the same principles applied locally. In the past many local Councils failed to be effective because busy clergy boycotted them, or gave them a low priority; others failed because those elected to them were 'fringe people' in the power structures of their own Churches. 'Churches Together' must bring together clergy and leading laity in a partnership of trust which becomes a day to day working relationship both formal and informal.

There should be a small but effective executive group which may include all the clergy and ministers who are in regular prayerful contact, supported by a larger body which meets formally perhaps only two or three times a year, though its members will meet in the course of their Church life and outreach very often. This bigger body (perhaps called 'The Assembly of Churches Together in Anytown') could have five members from larger Churches and two or three from the smaller, and could meet either residentially or at least for a full day. In some such way real friendships can be formed and the main directions mapped out by the Assembly, with the day to day running in the hands of the small executive.

This pattern should cut down the number of larger meetings, but when the Assembly meets there should be sufficient people present from every Church in the Local Covenant to ensure that its discussions and recommendations are truly representative. Some decisions will only be made after referral back to the individual Churches, but gradually as trust grows, more and more could be made by 'Churches Together' through their discussions at the Assembly.

The financing of corporate work in the area would probably be by a small regular levy for the running of 'Churches Together' itself, and larger levies on the individual Churches when it has been agreed that major projects should be undertaken in the name of all the Churches.

But we will attempt to deal with the most important area of all in the next chapter; namely what should be the main items on the agenda for such a body, and how that agenda of work for the Lord can be more effectively carried out by all the Churches together.

7

The Local Agenda

So just what does it all add up to? The Inter-Church Process 'Not Strangers But Pilgrims' has so far been a piece of history, some big meetings and a lot of structures. In this chapter I want to set out what it could amount to in practice at the local level. Clearly not everything can apply everywhere, but I am bold enough to suggest that there is something here for everyone wherever their Church is on the 'C Scale'.

One word of warning. In this chapter I am not so concerned with places where Churches have already united in single buildings and share most of their life, but with places where they are considering what should be the next practical step in local unity between a number of separate Churches. In this situation much of the life of each Church will continue as before, and much that is good will continue to be done by individual Churches. Most of our worship will continue in the pattern and manner we appreciate; much of the fellowship will continue in the life of each Church and its organisations. Most of the buildings will continue to be owned and financed by individual Churches. This may change as we learn to trust each other, and there must be a willingness to consider fundamental changes if these become necessary. It is the enemies of ecumenism who make out that unity obliterates the life of the individual Church. 'Small is beautiful' is a maxim welcomed by the Inter-Church Process, and may mean that quite small fellowships continue with their own life, but now in the context of being part of something bigger and more varied. Ecumenism should enlarge choice and not restrict it.

I want to set out the local agenda for such an area under six main headings:

1. Pastoral and evangelistic work
2. Service of the community
3. Publicity
4. Use of our buildings
5. Training local christians
6. Joint worship

There is bound to be some overlap as they are all aspects of local Church life which inter-relate with each other and are dependent on each other, especially in the area of training.

Pastoral and Evangelistic Work

The true end of ecumenism is mission, and this needs a very clear statement, especially as some of the more evangelical Churches have in the past stood aside from ecumenical structures seeing them as irrelevant to the effective proclamation of the Gospel. A good deal of large scale evangelism has in the past been 'non-denominational' in character, but in more recent years it has been more on a semi-ecumenical basis. It is interesting to see how Billy Graham has widened his basis of work, so that in some areas a wide range of Churches have taken part in his campaigns. However, there are still places where some Christian Churches are not accepted into evangelical partnership, and so instead of ecumenical mission there is only a working together of the theologically like-minded. Although changing, it is likely that the large scale evangelistic mission will continue, and it is to be hoped that the basis of such work will always be as wide as possible.

Local joint evangelism will probably have a different approach, and will have the advantage of working within a defined community. Later I give some examples of local ecumenical evangelistic missions, but first I want to show the great opportunities in the ongoing pastoral care which can unite different Churches in their outreach and care of the individual. God calls people to himself in a wide variety of ways, and no way is better or worse than another. If we are able to think of another tradition as part of 'us', rather than labelling it as 'them', we shall find many things we can share and also gain from each other.

The majority of people in our country have some knowledge of what the Christian faith is about, and if the popularity of the hymn 'The Lord is my Shepherd' at funerals and weddings is anything to go by, the concept of a 'caring Church' and a 'caring Gospel' is understood by most people, however tenuous their link with organised religion. Some feel badly let down by the Church, even though they never go near it, if there is no one on hand to show them practical care, sympathy, and help at times of personal crisis. In nearly forty years of general pastoral visiting in all sorts of communities I can hardly remember a dozen times that my concern has not been appreciated, and perhaps almost expected! The concept of the parson who knows everyone, and is always on hand, still exists even on a housing estate of twenty thousand people in which one family in seven moves every year!

Much fruitful evangelism begins with basic Christian love and care. But who is to give this pastoral care in large urban communities unless we are able to call on the total active membership of all Churches? The idea of it being the task of the clergy and ministers alone, is wrong in theory and impossible in practice, and some of the most rewarding ecumenical work is in schemes where local Churches of differing denominations share in the pastoral care of all 'parishioners'. In the past this has been seen as the exclusive role of the parish church, and other Churches with a more eclectic membership and theology, have either held off or not felt able to take part. Those Church members who think that they 'employ' a minister just to care for them, will need a good deal of education to enable them to see that in fact

Church members are themselves the carers in conjunction with their minister. Here then, is one field of activity crying out for a group of Churches to work out together how best to serve the individual needs of their local community. The Methodist practice of allocating each member to the care of a class leader can be developed to include care of those who are not regular church-goers. This is increasingly the pattern of local Methodist Churches and can be shared with others.

Once the local structure of the Churches has been defined as suggested in the last chapter, this may be one of the first joint projects to be considered. The scheme now to be described would need considerable adaptation in most areas, but is working well in places with a population of between five and twenty-five thousand. A village usually does not need a structure, but any community above a couple of thousand probably does. The scheme can have a number of titles but here I refer to it as a Road Steward Scheme.

The object is to have a Church member in every road, part of a road or block of flats, who is commissioned by the Churches to have pastoral charge of their area. This could well involve hundreds of people taking part as road stewards in a large area, and the element of basic training is important both at the launching of the scheme, and for keeping enthusiasm going. An actual service of commissioning for all who are going to take part is essential: if lay people are to act in the name of the local Churches, they must know what they are doing, and that they have been commissioned to their work in the name of Jesus Christ and his Church.

An initial Church survey of the area in which the scheme will operate will soon reveal that the ideal of a steward in every road can rarely be achieved. In Swindon we had one road with nearly twenty-five people, any of whom would have made a splendid steward, and about forty roads without a single possible person from any of our Churches! It is these roads that most need a Christian presence, and this can help us pinpoint our main areas of future mission.

I have often heard the remark, 'I'm afraid we are all very weak on the Council estate.' In some places where all the Churches together have very few members, such a scheme may seem quite impossible. But it can be started where there are members who are willing to share in this work and even if we cannot cover the whole area we should do what we can and hope and pray it will grow.

The size of area which can effectively be covered by one steward, depends partly on the person, and partly on the area itself. The most difficult areas are the large blocks of flats where people may be dead for a week without anyone knowing, and main roads where heavy traffic prevents much growth of neighbourliness and concern. As a rough guide, stewards can have some knowledge of about forty houses. Those who have small children or dogs have a wider knowledge of their neighbours than those without!

Once the scheme has been set up and the area to be covered defined, it is up to each Church taking part to put forward names and addresses of those who can be approached to help. This may include members of other Churches who worship outside the area, but who live within it. When a map has been drawn up and possible families identified, a large meeting can be called to launch the scheme and explain how it could work and people be invited to consider being trained for the work and then commissioned. Experience shows that about eighty per cent of those approached will agree as long as they understand what they are being asked to do, and what they are not. It is not a Neighbourhood Watch Scheme (though it could well relate to one) nor is it just a Good Neighbour Scheme for the elderly, though again it could relate to such an existing scheme. The aim is to make sure that all the people who live there, and those who move in as newcomers, know that their local Churches are united in offering friendship and care, and want to invite them to be part of the local Christian community in its varying Churches and fellowships. But above all their task is to be Christ: be his hands and his feet in the place where they live and to show the same compassion and care that he shows us, pointing people to him as the source of all our caring.

That is a tall order and it will not always be achieved; some people who take it on are either too frightened or forgetful to do anything; others have to be restrained from trying to run their road on military lines, and others again have to learn that their task is caring and not prying! There are real risks in setting up such a scheme, but if the training and the inspiration are right, the rewards will be very great.

But one word of caution. A scheme such as this which involves many lay people will make big demands on the local ministerial team in terms of the individual stewards who begin to grow in their faith, and of following up the contacts which they make. Nothing can kill enthusiasm faster than not taking up the openings created by the stewards, and the feeling 'I've told him three times that the new people at 47 are Methodists, and still no one has called' will soon destroy all the initial enthusiasm. A really active laity requires a very responsible and responsive hard-working ministry.

Each community will work out variations to such a scheme, and probably add to it some sort of Christian Care scheme which enables people with cars, skills or time, to help in particular cases. No one can do everything, so both the ministerial team and the road stewards need other Church members to call on for help. Sometimes this can be provided by members who do not reside in the area. A Baptist steward calling on an Anglican family and providing help in some practical form by a Roman Catholic, teaches more about ecumenism in action than many a conference. Living the Gospel together in the places where we live is the keystone of local ecumenism and mission.

I would contend that this ongoing pastoral care provides the basis for the most effective form of friendship evangelism, if those who are involved are able to give a reason for their faith. However, there are many other forms that local pastoral care and evangelism can take where an ecumenical approach is almost certainly the most effective. I would mention just a few by way of example:

* The 'Faith in Print' scheme, whereby local Churches pay for good, selected, and readable Christian literature to be placed in their public library for people to borrow, has proved very successful in well over two hundred places.

* The holding of open air processions and dramas such as the joint Passion Play in Lowestoft which, after eighteen months of work, brought together three hundred performers from every Church in the town to be watched by 2,500 people.

* The promotion of joint Flower Festivals which encourage people to visit a wide variety of decorated local churches linked together with a unifying Christian theme.

* A town or village fête sponsored by all the Churches with a common purpose and perhaps a common appeal for Christian Aid, Tear Fund or some other ecumenical work here or abroad.

The list can be almost endless and all are better undertaken together than apart. The wider the variety of Churches involved the greater the appeal. We do not all come to accept the invitation of Christ in the same way. This must be part of our shared message to our community.

There are also a number of local ecumenical missions in which the various traditions can join in publicising a variety of mission events and so make clear the multiform nature of our approach to God. A few examples from different parts of Britain will best illustrate this.

* The 1988 Chislehurst Churches Festival of Faith which began after the Lent '86 course when people realised that they were often afraid to share their faith. The Anglican, Methodist and Roman Catholic Churches worked together for eighteen months planning the Festival which lasted two weeks with the aim, 'To provide an opportunity for the Christians of Chislehurst to demonstrate their unity in Christ and to share their faith with others as well as giving people a chance to consider the relevance of the Christian Faith today.' Festival leaders came from all the denominations and over three hundred local people were involved with a budget of eight thousand pounds. Every group was catered for and every Church made its own distinctive

contribution, and the comment was 'the Churches of Chislehurst will never be the same again'.

* A totally different event was the Churches' involvement in the Glasgow Garden Festival where in co-operation with the Christian Enquiry Agency in Scotland, several thousands of requests were received for further help in response to the worship and witness of the Churches at that great event. Other Festivals planned will have similar 'Churches Together' initiatives working alongside, and within these events.

* In Enfield, London, the Local Ecumenical Project launched Joint Outreach Youth (JOY) and all seven Churches worked on a Youth Mission which combined some joint events and some in the individual Churches, each co-ordinated and jointly promoted. The team worked closely with schools and clubs and the Gospel was preached and enacted in many unusual ways and places. Not everything worked and there were some disappointments, but the end product was a number of young people who committed their lives to Christ, and also a much closer working together of all the Churches' young people.

* A large group of Churches in South Manchester worked together in 'United in the City' and it was notable in bringing together some Churches which were mainly white in membership, and others mainly black. Their experience after a variety of mission events was that 'it has changed a whole climate of thought between our Churches which have traditionally not necessarily been over tolerant of one another at grass-roots level.' In a summary of their work they went on to stress how important it was to build up trust between the Churches taking part and added, 'We felt that evangelism should be rooted in more local events, perhaps incorporating two or three neighbouring Churches, but also that we should broaden our scope to incorporate other areas of local need, where together we might achieve what alone was beyond us.' I cannot think of a more positive local affirmation of the Swanwick Declaration than that.

* In Edinburgh, 'There is Hope' was a campaign of many Churches which had the purpose of 'encouraging Christians

to pray together for Revival, providing a framework for Churches to develop their own witness while working simultaneously with other Churches, and communicating the message of Christ to every person.' They go on to say, 'While written materials for "There is Hope" will emphasise truths that are central to most Churches, there is no intention to try and establish detailed agreement on all points of theology or practice.' These are the new and encouraging notes being sounded by a truly ecumenical mission which can rejoice in differences but combine in proclamation.

* Dronfield is just starting to plan a possible joint mission to the town in 1992 by all the Covenanted Churches, and may consider using the 'Barnabas Initiative' planned by the Bible Society Church Training Group. 'The Barnabas Initiative has many features which reflect the character and ministry of Barnabas as related in the Acts of the Apostles. It encourages groups of Churches to work together in mission. It provides a framework upon which a group of Churches can build their local evangelistic effort and plan their future mission strategy. It provides positive help and advice for building effective relationships between different Churches and between you and your community.'

Ever since the days of 'Call to the North' and then Archbishop Donald Coggan's 'Nationwide Initiative in Evangelism' (NIE) at the end of the seventies, a group has been working on just such examples and encouraging such schemes. Much of the wisdom learnt in this is distilled in the BCC booklet of 1988, *Telling the Good News Together*. In the third section of the report it says, 'Shared evangelism has practical gains; it is a witness to the Lordship of Christ. People's comments make this clear — "We'd never have expected you people to be working together!" It can open doors which were closed to individual churches; some schools, factories and civic authorities that have resisted denominational approaches have been known to welcome ecumenical teams that demonstrate the co-operation of local churches. Instead of seeming to say, "God will love you if you conform to our tradition", evangelising together proclaims that Churches are sharing together the same God of love who sent his only Son.'

Service of the Community

Much that has been said under the first heading is relevant to the Churches serving their community, but in this section I want to deal with ways in which 'Churches Together' can serve through co-operation with statutory and voluntary community agencies. By definition these agencies cannot favour one denomination more than another and statutory bodies especially find difficulty in working with a divided and seemingly competing and uncoordinated range of Churches.

But if the Churches can combine and present a united front, most agencies are only too happy to work with them. They appreciate that the Churches are capable of much greater experiment and have resources of man and woman power greater than any other group in society. The present government policy is to depend more and more on the voluntary working with, or even taking over, some aspects of the community care programme and such co-operation will be even more vital in the future.

There are many examples of the Churches working together to pioneer half-way homes for discharged mental patients or ex-offenders; and drug addiction, alcoholism, and AIDS offer areas for close co-operation. While one Church may undertake such a venture, it is much more likely to be effective if tackled jointly.

There are probably thousands of Church-based Luncheon Clubs, open house coffee bars and pre-school playgroups. I will refer to these again in connection with the use of church buildings. Many groups of Churches play a most useful part in setting up community meetings at lunch-time for all involved in social care so that clergy, teachers, police, social, probation and medical workers can have an informal opportunity to meet and share common concerns.

Against this general background of Church care I want to highlight Church relationships with two groups in particular. First the medical profession and then the teaching profession.

The medical profession has undergone startling changes, and is faced with new moral problems almost every year. 'Churches Together' could well play a part by trying to assemble an informal clergy and doctor group. It might be wider than the title suggests and incorporate others in the medical professions. This can be of great help to all who deal with true health of body, mind and spirit. Guest speakers and discussion can be very helpful. Not all doctors are Christians, but most are willing to give careful thought to moral problems and the spiritual side of healing. I have a vivid recollection of thirty years ago, at a Bristol clergy and doctor group, when a junior woman-doctor shared with us a complete vision – namely a place where people could die with dignity and with little suffering. We all felt a personal involvement and responsibility to help Dr Cicely Saunders found St Christopher's Hospice, and then to take part in the great burgeoning of the hospice movement. Within one generation a dream has become a reality in scores of places. Here was an area of true co-operation which has changed the life and death of hundreds of thousands of people.

The other profession which has seen profound and often disturbing changes is teaching. As with the medical profession the percentage of Christian teachers is probably about the same as in other walks of life, but again there are quite a large number of non-Christian teachers who have to give religious and moral teaching, and are happy to discuss it and its implications for their pupils. Some way by which the Churches and those who teach in the same area can come together to share problems and joys can be very helpful, and a number of ecumenical bodies have helped to set up such local meetings.

Especially since the recent 1989 Education Act there has been a growing opportunity for the Churches to be more involved in schools themselves, and any community which can field an ecumenical team of ministers and qualified laity to help in schools with assemblies, would be welcomed with open arms by many, though not all Head Teachers. Having myself always worked in ecumenical situations where about three quarters of all state primary and secondary schools welcomed us on a regular basis, I am saddened to find that in many towns and cities the contact between the Churches and the schools is very slim, or even non-existent. With the renewed emphasis on a 'Christian assembly' many Heads have turned to local Churches for help, and while not all clergy and ministers are capable of this important work, there is no doubt that the opportunity of such contacts is invaluable.

Even if the teaching content of a ten-minute assembly cannot be very great, the fact that our faces are known by every child in the area is of great pastoral value. The Free Church Federal Council has recently published a short leaflet called *Worship in County Schools* which has many valuable suggestions for those undertaking this work. It can be very demanding, as we know here in our own town where the team ministry has regular entry into eight of our eleven schools. In one secondary school a team of clergy and laity are invited in once a term and for a fortnight not only take school assembly with 1,200 children, but year assemblies and class assemblies too! Although we have only about thirty at a time in a class it is a great joy to have immediate and open come-back on what you said in the school assembly. I always come away from my mornings in school with a deep sense of gratitude for the opportunities given us, and a profound respect for the teaching profession who keep it up all the year round!

Contact with the schools, both Church and State, can be of great value in the total ministry of the Churches to their community. The work that clergy, ministers and lay people can do on the increasingly important Governing Bodies, though far from easy, can bear often very unexpected fruit. Also related to our schools are the fairly new Community Education Councils, and these provide opportunities for biblical and other adult study courses to be run and financed by the Local Authority, as well as valuable links into many areas of adult education including work with the handicapped.

The Churches have more allies in the community than most people realise, but, if we are to work with them, we must have the humility to learn from them, and to earn our place rather than demand it by right. I would emphasise that when working with our community the only sensible, or possible way to do it is as 'Churches Together'.

Publicity

By far the best form of publicity is the quality of life and love that Christians and Churches show in their homes, communities, places of work and leisure. But this needs to be supplemented by organised forms of publicity which tell people what Christians believe and how they express this in their lives. Until recently our family used to take holidays on the English canals, and progress is so unpredictable that we could never plan where we would be able to worship on a Sunday. I recall a number of fruitless visits to canal-side Churches on a Saturday evening; fruitless because they gave no indication of when the Christians there worshipped or even if they ever did! I expect the regulars knew, but the impression those Churches gave us was that they were either closed, or did not expect anyone ever to be interested in joining with them!

Publicity should declare, 'We are alive and we are here to welcome visitors.' There are few permanent communities in our country today; people on average move house once every seven years, and we constantly need new ways of making known the life and practice of our Churches, and sharing this information as widely as possible. Publicity must be the Churches speaking together and telling the world what we are and what we do. Publicity by one Church alone will be seen as competing with, rather than complementing, others.

A growing custom is for the Church notice boards in a town or area to have some overall title like 'Churches Together in Our Town' and underneath the denomination and the details of services etc. It is also good if the Churches can devise some symbol which can be used on everything published by the Churches, which at once speaks both of the locality and the Churches together which serve it.

Despite the growing number of free distribution newspapers (which can themselves be excellent ways of showing how the Churches are witnessing together) there are far more local Church publications. These vary greatly in appearance and value, but represent a way of getting into more homes than those of Church attenders. Many are magazines or newspapers representing all the Churches of the area, but the increased circulation and shared talent could improve them considerably. There is a great number of excellent publications such as that produced by the Council of Churches in Leek.

At one time in the West of England in an ecumenical paper called *Contact* we had about a hundred different Churches working together in local editions and reaching many thousands of homes. Finance defeated it after seven years, but it showed what could be done. A good ecumenical magazine or paper which reflects the life of the Churches and the community can reach nearly half the homes, provided there is a good team of distributors who believe in what they are doing. A useful way of doing this is to unite a Road Steward Scheme with magazine distribution so that newcomers are offered news of the Churches as soon as they arrive. It is encouraging to see how many Churches who combine to produce a monthly or quarterly magazine for the homes of the area, also have separate free weekly news sheets for their Church members to complement it.

If a joint magazine or paper seems too ambitious, a free leaflet or invitation at Christmas, Easter and Harvest put into every house in the town or village can perform something of the same function. Another advantage of combined publicity is that it justifies purchasing better equipment such as word processors and photocopiers. A Church Office where all this shared equipment can be stored and used and material be produced can be invaluable. While some large individual Churches may be able to afford expensive equipment it is beyond the reach of smaller Churches.

The place of local radio in Christian publicity should not need underlining. It is true that in the nineties there is going to be something of a shake up, but the advent of more community radio could be of great help to local Churches. Ever since the coming of local radio over twenty-five years ago the Churches have worked closely together in this medium and some of the very best ecumenical work has taken place in BBC and Independent Local Radio studios. The Association of Christians in Local Broadcasting is probably the broadest and most ecumenical body in our country, and has done a lot to encourage and train Christians to play a part in this section of the media. It is a fact that, without this co-operation from over fifty radio stations, Lent '86 and the subsequent Lent courses would never have taken place. Yet many Churches are still not using the facilities made available to them through local radio. A short two-minute interview recently put out on BBC Radio Sheffield produced far more constructive response in my locality, than most of my sermons!

The Churches need publicity and the best way of obtaining it is by showing that they are working as one in presenting the Good News, but doing so in a number of ways and forms which reflect the variety of Christian experience in any community.

Use of Our Buildings

During my seven years as Archdeacon of Rochester I had to spend a good deal of time on buildings, dealing with both their preservation and their use, and I was known to say that I favoured an association for the encouragement of church tents and the abolition of permanent buildings! We are at our most denominational when we are in our own church buildings and the very architecture of most of the older buildings speaks of our brand of religion. Inside we are surrounded by the High Altar or the High Pulpit; the sprinkling font or the full-dip one; the banners of the Virgin Mary and the saints, or of the Sunday School anniversary. Almost everything speaks of our own tradition and much that we value. But our buildings also speak of the high cost of keeping warm and dry, and so often absorb a great part of our giving, concern and energies.

In *Views from the Pews* after Lent '86, many groups mentioned how much freer they felt, when meeting in 'neutral homes' rather than in denominational buildings, to discuss their views and listen to those of others. It is probably true that some of the best ecumenical work is done outside churches rather than inside. But things are changing, and while people still have a great affection for their own buildings, television services have helped to acquaint them with buildings for worship other than their own, and people's increased mobility should enable a wider knowledge of the variety of buildings and the worship of God that is offered in them.

Many of our great churches such as Abbeys and Cathedrals are now used regularly for ecumenical services or indeed host those of other denominations who rightly look to them as a 'mother church'. It would not have been possible thirty years ago for the Inaugural Service of the United Reformed Church to take place in Westminster Abbey as it did in 1972, and it is interesting that on that day the legal constituting of the new Church took place across the road in the Methodist Central Hall! Although still largely administered by the Church of England our historic Cathedrals are seen as places of pilgrimage and worship by all Christians, and Derby Cathedral was the first to become part of a Local Ecumenical Project. In the newly built Coventry Cathedral after the war, there was a Chapel of Unity, but perhaps the change is that now we see the whole Cathedral as a place of unity and like Derby, it too is a member of a Local Ecumenical Project.

In many hundreds of places there are shared churches, and this has brought change. In the United Church at Hemel Hempstead, shared by the Anglicans, Baptist and Roman Catholics, the Stations of the Cross in collage were designed by a local Salvationist! Not all shared churches have worked well and some are more united than others. Sharing can mean no more than complaining that the last lot didn't put away the coffee cups or the chalice. Congregations that live under the same roof but have not yet got 'married' may need to look again at the way they work, but there are splendid examples of Churches working together in and through one main building, often sharing a completely integrated life. Others still maintain some denominational worship and life but increasingly are united in many weekday activities.

Often in new areas the shared building has to double up as church and community hall, and the United Church at the centre of Skelmersdale in Lancashire is but one example of a church fully integrated with its local community. It is said that it has more people passing through its doors in any one week than many a Cathedral!

The new Church of England Ecumenical Canons are helpful over the use of Church of England buildings, and the Sharing of Church Buildings Act, though not without its problems, enables genuine partnership. The closure of any church building is a very traumatic event and in some cases, as we have seen, the rationalisation of church buildings need not lead to closure but to a wider and different use. Another fairly new approach to the use of our buildings is when the local community takes over part of a large older church for use as a library, clinic or day centre, keeping other parts available for worship. Once a real degree of trust has been built up and people are used to being in and out of each other's premises, and start to think of them as 'ours' and not 'theirs', all sorts of things become possible.

Any local grouping of Churches would be well advised to consider the joint use of all their church buildings. Church halls and old schools can be of great importance and a common approach to their use and equipment can add to their usefulness and value. The co-operative use of halls has meant that hundreds, if not thousands, are in daily use for the local community as Day Centres, Advice Centres, and Luncheon Clubs for the elderly and handicapped. In Nottinghamshire I especially remember visiting a town centre Methodist church which had been rebuilt, so that part of it formed an excellent charity shop in the market place.

In the Ecumenical Parish of Swindon Old Town, we carried out a complete survey of our four halls, and because we held them in common, were able to reorganise and re-equip them. The big old Victorian parish hall was turned into a Day Centre, run by volunteers from the Churches, in co-operation with the local psychiatric hospital. It was completely modernised with a grant from the local authority. This resulted in a much better hall for Church use in the evenings and at weekends, but that day-time users had to move out to meet round the corner at the Methodist hall. The URC hall was equipped as a special hall for physically handicapped people and another Anglican hall as our main youth building. We were quite convinced that by being joint stewards of all our property, we were more truly serving God and the local community.

Buildings are the most visible and expensive part of Church life, and a joint approach to their use for the Church and the community is an essential item for a local Church agenda.

Training Local Christians

It is hard to think of any aspect of Christian training that could not be carried out better with other Churches. Some of the residential theological colleges and almost all the non-residential training courses are now ecumenical, and more lay courses are planned for a very wide range of Churches and their members. Often a single Church may have only one or two people for training for some specialist purpose and they may have to travel far for their courses. If, however, the Churches in an area are sharing training there may well be enough members for the course to be held locally with all the advantages that flow from that.

Christian training will increasingly be the basis of much shared local work, and Lent '86 showed a great appetite for such training provided it is at a level and of a type that ordinary lay people can appreciate. The most important training is in basic Christian beliefs and practices. We can no longer take for granted a Christian home or school background, and so the Churches themselves must accept the responsibility to provide Christian nurture and training at the local level as a matter of course. It must be provided for all age groups from the youngest to the oldest, and it is encouraging to note how many people are coming to full faith in Jesus Christ later in life. The concept that there is a certain age at which you should be confirmed or converted is dying fast, and in the Church of England, as in other Churches, adult commitment is growing and our traditional approach to Christian training must change to reflect this.

Children's work will continue to be important, however, both for our children and for their parents. Much Sunday School work will take place in the individual Church, but the training of teachers and the encouragement of them in occasional larger events which draw together the children and their teachers from all the local Churches is most important. Joint open air services, parades, walks, rambles and processions are practical and enjoyable ways to bring all ages and Churches together. In a Midlands town recently, the five local Churches had a walk of witness around the five places of worship, and as well as Sunday School, the Boys' and Girls' Brigades, Scouts and Guides took part. We don't need to talk to children about ecumenism – let them act it out.

With the secondary school student, joint training becomes even more important. In the first place, some Churches do not have many children in this age group in their midst, and it is important that in the fairly 'unchristian' atmosphere of most secondary schools, youngsters should know their fellow Christians. Where local Churches are working together, much of the teenage work, and especially the Church membership or confirmation training, can be done on a joint basis. This is especially true of Local Ecumenical Projects which follow up the training course with a joint Confirmation and Reception into Full Membership service, which admits the new members into membership of all the participating Churches.

In Swindon our four Churches worked out a joint three-year course called 'Quest' which was run together for all our young people aged between twelve and sixteen. A short account of it which I wrote was asked for by hundreds of other areas, and it is good to know that Quest groups exist in many towns nearly twenty years later. Its essence is simple. It is a basic course of Christian teaching and experience which brings together a team of adults from all the Churches to work with a team of youngsters. It includes some features of a confirmation course combined with a form of youth club, but one which allows people to grow in faith as they go along, and be confirmed when they feel ready, rather than being forced into a mould. I don't believe one Church, however large, can, by itself, provide the resources either of teenagers or the varied team of leaders. A great emphasis on residential work is a key part of the Quest concept, and the title speaks of the approach shared with younger Christians.

Despite all that we hear about the problems of marriage, the institution itself is thriving, and while most marriages still take place in the Church of England, the preparation for all Church marriages can be undertaken by Churches working together. There are many models ranging from large courses worked out with the help of marriage organisations like 'Relate', to small informal house groups where a married couple meet with a few couples about to launch out on marriage. There is no perfect model, but the urgent need for both careful marriage preparation and for the support of couples after marriage needs no underlining with the statistic of forty per cent break-up of recent marriages. We now have the additional responsibility of the preparation and pastoral care of couples whose first marriage has broken up, but who seek to re-marry and remain practising Christians. All our Churches face this challenge whatever our rules are about re-marriage in Church.

Because marriage preparation can be very local, it is more likely to be successful run by an ecumenical group, rather than by an Anglican deanery or Methodist circuit. In Dronfield we have Baptists and Roman Catholics who are helping Anglicans prepare couples for the ups and downs of matrimonial life. If future husbands and wives can learn from different local Christians that we do not all think or act exactly alike, we may have taught them a most important lesson for marriage and life!

There are thus many aspects of ministry that need local courses to train the trainers and helpers. One of the best schemes I have known is in the field of bereavement counselling at a local level run by a group of Churches. A small number of bereaved members were themselves first trained how to use their own bereavement, and then went on to use their experiences to help others. There are so many instances where this work has led to faith, that everywhere we need such schemes whereby those who have experience and training can share with others. The realisation that the person who can help others most, is one who has also been through that particular experience has led to a rapid growth of organisations of a 'self help' variety. When I was chaplain of a large maternity hospital and I got the call that a Down's syndrome baby had arrived, I knew at once how limited my role would be, but just how much help could be provided from a small group of Christian parents who had been through that particular agony.

If the 'Churches Together' decide to set up some form of Road Steward Scheme I have already stressed the importance of training. This should include training in how to approach people, knowledge of the Churches and community, and some knowledge of how to care for people in an emergency. Most important of all is to know when they themselves should call for help from others.

In addition to these specific trainings there is the ongoing task of helping people to grow in the faith and love of God. People do now realise that a six week confirmation course at the age of fourteen and a sermon once or twice a month, does not teach them everything there is to know about Jesus Christ and his faith! The trouble is that most ministers, working by themselves, just have not the time for organising sustained teaching courses; but if they link up with others and share the load within the ecumenical team and area, ready to use the many varied resources of the diocese and districts, good teaching groups can be formed and we can have the joy of seeing Christians of all ages and backgrounds growing in their faith and its practice.

The national ecumenical Lent courses run in 1986, 1988 and 1990 and others run locally may seem to be becoming more important ecumenical events than the Week of Prayer. I would be sorry if this meant less prayer, because we need more prayer rather than less. But I must welcome the growth of the Lent groups, as without them it is unlikely that the Churches would have reached the position of launching the next stage of 'Not Strangers But Pilgrims'. It was interesting to read the 1986 reports and see how much value lay people put on these small house groups, but how much less useful they were when organised by one Church on its own.

There are enough aspects of all forms of joint training to fill many an agenda for the local Churches, but they would be wise to set up a sub-group just to deal with this aspect of local ecumenical work.

Joint Worship

The order of the agenda in this chapter is not of great significance, because all the headings are important and overlap one another. But I have deliberately left worship and especially public worship until last. In my four years as Home Secretary of the Church of England Board of Mission and Unity when I spent most of my time 'on the road' (or more accurately on British Rail) I visited many local councils and projects, and I was interested to see how the first things people talked about were the joint services that they held. I am certain that joint worship is of great importance and certainly in the 1987 conferences it played a crucial part as we have seen.

But I do not believe we should judge the value of local ecumenism by how many joint services are held, and it may be more important to look first to 'joint service', rather than 'joint services'. In some types of Local Ecumenical Projects, it may be that all worship is joint. Certainly there are hundreds of places where there is only one act of Sunday worship, which has been constructed to bring together people and insights of different traditions, who now accept it as their own. But many more Christians have their main diet of worship in denominational buildings using denominational prayer and hymn books. The fact that the prayer books are now much more 'Common Prayer' to all is important, and hymns would be a great unifying factor if only they had the same tunes!

In the past not all joint services have furthered the cause of Church unity, and I can remember occasions after united services on cold January evenings when people rejoiced to get back to their own round of familiar worship. Partly this was because of unfamiliarity with each other's churches, and the different ways of doing things, but another aspect is that some services ended up as the lowest common denomination of worship lacking any character or distinction.

The determination at the Swanwick Conference that there should be a mix of ecumenical with eucharistic worship rooted in each of the major traditions was clearly a crucial decision. The same lesson should be learnt at the local level. While we should use some ecumenical worship (such as the Week of Prayer and the May Christian Aid Service which have been carefully prepared to enlarge our vision and lift us from parochial concerns), for the most part our joint worship should be one Church holding its best characteristic worship, but making certain that all who are there understand what is happening, and as far as possible are invited to join in. In this way we can begin to value each other's traditions, and share each other's treasures of liturgy, hymnology and prayer. If after taking part in such a service, we can meet to discuss the shared experience and realise again the truth that 'to be different is not to be wrong', we shall have grown in worship and spirituality.

On the 'Churches Together' agenda under the heading of worship, there should also be careful planning for joint worship in the open air, with such events as Good Friday processions, Whit Sunday acts of witness and holiday time services on beaches or parks. Festivals are a growing part of local life in most communities and joint worship should be part of them.

Worship should not always be thought of in terms of the big service or event; much of the best ecumenical worship is in small prayer groups or informal healing services. These may be held in church or home, formal or informal, and they become the place where we meet as Christians and leave our denominational labels at the front door. Prayer for one another and for the needs of Christ's Church and the world he came to save is at its most effective in such a setting where we are simply united by the presence of Christ himself.

There will be other items to add to the local ecumenical agenda, but these six main headings should be enough to be going on with! Surely this list should convince us beyond any doubt that we need a way of working together at every level, and that such structures have their place, as long as the agenda is real, and comes off the paper and into the life and witness of every Church and its members.

POSTSCRIPT

In a Changing World

Since I started writing this book in July 1989 the world has changed, and it is clear that 1989 will equal 1789 as 'a year of Revolution'. The events of this past twelve months in Russia, Czechoslovakia, Germany, Hungary, Poland, Romania and South Africa are so momentous and astonishing that few of us can even begin to see what our world will look like at the end of next year, let alone at the end of the century.

It will be a different world and it could be a better one. Human nature has not radically changed, but political and social structures have collapsed even more completely than walls. The visual impression is of tens of thousands of people packed into square after square all waving banners with one message – Freedom.

Behind much of the new 'spring' in Eastern Europe and South Africa there lies Christian experience and faith, and an understanding of Christ's death and resurrection as being reflected in, and making sense of our world.

To the considerable surprise of many in the more secular West, in country after country it has been the Christian Churches which have nurtured and kept alive faith and hope in freedom, under whatever banner or title it has been proclaimed. Almost every branch of the Christian Church has played its part; the Roman Catholic Church in Poland, the Lutherans in East Germany, the Protestant and Catholic in Romania, the Orthodox and Baptist in Russia, and further afield the Anglican and the Pentecostal Churches in South Africa. In time we shall also find the vital role of the minority

Christian Church in China. Not all Christians are strong enough to witness in this way, but priests, ministers and lay people have been prepared to stand up for their beliefs which were grounded not just in politics or nationalism, but in a common belief in a God of justice and freedom, who cares deeply about the world he has made.

That the Christian religion was something many people were prepared to witness to, and indeed die for, came as a considerable surprise and rebuke to other parts of the world which thought that God had been safely relegated to the religious extremities of life, or totally dismissed as a relic from the past. Religion has proved that it is not an 'opium of the people' but a strength of the people which has outlasted its rivals.

Against this large international backcloth the events of 'Not Strangers But Pilgrims' may seem somewhat small and insignificant, but they can also be seen as reflecting something of these changes and also contributing something important to this worldwide movement of the Spirit – whether we call the Spirit 'Holy' or not.

The ecumenical movement in this century, and especially in the past decade, has been seeking to find new ways of showing unity in Christ which values both the unity and the diversity of our experience of God. We know now that uniformity is out; unity in diversity is in. As Christians we are coming to rejoice in a wide diversity within the basic oneness of our faith and can accept that 'to be different is not to be wrong'.

As the twentieth century has gone on we have been forced to accept that we all live in one quite small inhabited world (*Oikumenia*), and within it we are dependent on one another for our very survival. No one part of the body can dispense with any other. But this realisation, far from levelling us down to a monochrome existence, has in fact heightened our racial and national consciousness in almost every community. Each of us is proud to affirm our nationality, ethnic origins, customs and languages – and our religious faith.

Look at 'Not Strangers But Pilgrims' against this

background and the principles it has been trying to articulate become vitally important and relevant. It can make a real contribution to a world trying to find a new way of living together, when it affirms both the brotherhood of all mankind, and loyalty to family, Church, race or nation. It is keeping these two different strands in harmony that is so essential. It is far from easy, yet it must be part of 'the ministry of reconciliation' that Christians offer in today's changing world.

But if after so many past centuries of inter-Christian conflict and internal squabbling, we now dare to offer others a pattern of united Christian witness, we have to move fast if present 'deeds' are to speak as loud as past 'words'. The remark, 'See how these Christians love one another' has been too often said in sarcasm or bitterness rather than admiration or envy.

'Churches Together' is seeking to show that Christians of very different backgrounds in theology, race and politics can live together in harmony, and actively work with each other to proclaim that 'Jesus is Lord'. Lest it be thought that this new spirit is peculiar to Britain these are words from the 1989 Manila Mission Conference (Lausanne II), 'We affirm the urgent need for Churches, mission agencies and other Christian organisations, to co-operate in evangelism and social action, repudiating competition and avoiding duplication.' Moving up the 'C Scale' is Christian policy throughout the world!

Those of us who have been actively involved in 'Not Strangers But Pilgrims' are convinced that 'Churches Together' gives us all a new opportunity to move forward in common action and concern 'at all levels and in all places'. In this book I have mainly stressed the importance of local action because that is where I have been most involved, but it must also happen at all other levels as well.

In my introduction I said I had written this book mainly for those of us who took part in Lent '86. If that million people can now be encouraged to try and apply the lessons learnt from 'Not Strangers But Pilgrims', the Christian pattern of life and witness in our country can significantly change for the better before the end of this century. If we can show in word and deed that our unity in Jesus Christ is such that, while we continue to rejoice in our differences, they do not hinder us from a common declaration that 'Jesus Christ is Lord', then we have something of lasting value and importance to offer to everyone in our rapidly changing world.

Jesus is Lord, and it is his world in which we live and not ours; we have it on trust from him to use wisely and share with all his children, however different all of us may be.

Lord God, we thank you,
for calling us into the company
of those who trust in Christ,
and seek to obey his will.
May your Spirit guide and strengthen us,
in mission and service to your world:
For we are strangers no longer,
But pilgrims together on the way to your Kingdom.

For Further Reading

Not Strangers But Pilgrims Publications

Reflections (How Churches View their life and Mission)
Observations on the Church from Britain and Abroad
Views from the Pews: Lent '86 and Local Ecumenism
What on Earth is the Church For?
Churches Together in Pilgrimage
Don't Just Co-operate − You're Commited!

These are joint publications of British Council of Churches and Catholic Truth Society

British Council of Churches and Consultative Committee for Local Ecumenical Projects in England Publications

Telling the Good News Together
Christian Unity in the Village
*Local Church Unity: Guidelines for Local Ecumenical Projects and
    Sponsoring Bodies*
Constitutional Guidelines for a Local Ecumenical Project
Stewards of God's House
Ministry in Local Ecumenical Projects
A Guidebook for Sponsoring Bodies and Ecumenical Councils
Guidelines to the Sharing of Church Buildings Act
Together on the Way by Chris Ellis
A Handbook of Church Administration by Basil Hazledine
    (Autumn 1990)

Church of England Publications

Ecumenical Relations: Canons B43 and B44 and Code of Practice
The Measure of Mission (BMU)
Towards a Theology for Inter-faith Dialogue (BMU)

Roman Catholic Publications

Local Churches in Covenant
At Your Service

Other Books

A History of English Christianity, Adrian Hastings, London: Collins 1986.
Restoring the Kingdom, Andrew Walker, London: Hodder & Stoughton, 1985 & 1988.
Better Together, David Sheppard and Derek Worlock, London: Hodder & Stoughton, 1988.
Battered Bride?, David Winter, Eastbourne: Monarch Publications, 1988.
Sharing Communion, Ruth Reardon and Melania Finch, London: Collins, 1983 (out of print).

Addresses

Council of Churches for Britain and Ireland (C.C.B.I.),
Inter-Church House, 35–41 Lower Marsh, London SE1 7RL.

Churches Together in England (C.T.E.),
Inter-Church House, 35–41 Lower Marsh, London SE1 7RL.

Action of Churches Together in Scotland (ACTS),
Scottish Churches House, Dunblane, Perthshire FX15 0AJ.

Churches Together in Wales (CYTUN),
21 St Helens Rd, Swansea SA1 4AP.

The Irish Council of Churches,
Inter-Church Centre, 48 Elmwood Ave, Belfast BT9 6AZ.

Catholic Truth Society,
38–40 Eccleston Square, London SW1V 1PD.

Church of England Church House Bookshop,
Great Smith St, London SW1P 3BN.